You've GOT THIS!

HOW TO LOOK UP WHEN LIFE HAS YOU DOWN

You've GOT THIS!

HOW TO LOOK UP WHEN LIFE HAS YOU DOWN

AL CARRAWAY

CHAD HYMAS

WHITNEY WILCOX LAYCOCK

DALLAS LLOYD

HANK SMITH

TAMU SMITH

ZANDRA VRANES

CFI
AN IMPRINT OF CEDAR FORT, INC.
SPRINGVILLE, UTAH

ISBN 13: 978-1-4621-1942-4

Published by CFI, an imprint of Cedar Fort, Inc., 2373 W. 700 S., Springville, UT 84663
Distributed by Cedar Fort, Inc., www.cedarfort.com

LIBRARY OF CONGRESS CATALOGING-IN-PUBLICATION DATA

Names: Hahl, Elise, compiler.
Title: You've got this! : how to look up when life has you down / compiled by
  Elise Hahl.
Description: Springville, Utah : CFI, an imprint of Cedar Fort, Inc., [2016]
  | Includes bibliographical references and index.
Identifiers: LCCN 2016035566 (print) | LCCN 2016037899 (ebook) | ISBN
  9781462119424 (perfect bound : alk. paper) | ISBN 9781462127184 (epub,
  pdf, mobi)
Subjects: LCSH: Mormon youth--Religious life. | Mormon youth--Conduct of
  life. | LCGFT: Essays.
Classification: LCC BX8643.Y6 Y68 2016 (print) | LCC BX8643.Y6 (EBOOK)
  | DDC
  248.8/30882893--DC23
LC record available at https://lccn.loc.gov/2016035566

Cover design by Shawnda T. Craig
Cover design © 2016 by Cedar Fort, Inc.
Edited and typeset by Chelsea Holdaway

Printed in the United States of America

10 9 8 7 6 5 4 3 2 1

Printed on acid-free paper

CONTENTS

INTRODUCTION

Elise Hahl

This is a collection of stories that's meant to give you strength to deal with your greatest challenges.

A lot of you are already on board with that, so welcome. But some of you aren't so sure how any of this applies to *you*. After all, what do you know about navigating life in a wheelchair, like Chad Hymas; or playing in the Rose Bowl, like Dallas Lloyd? Maybe you haven't joined the Church to the disappointment of your family, like Al Carraway; moved to a foreign country, like Whitney Laycock; lost all your junior-high friends, like Tamu Smith; or dealt with a senile gentleman in your pew shouting out Hallelujahs at random moments during sacrament meeting, like Zandra Vranes. Maybe Joseph in Egypt lived too many millennia ago to be relevant to you, no matter how many neat insights Hank Smith shares about his life, and no matter how hilarious Joseph's narrative becomes in Zandra's version of the story.

But you know what? When you face a challenge, you'll be surprised by how well you remember the wisdom in this book. You'll recall how the gospel helped each of these individuals to pull through and be happy. You'll see that just as there was hope for them, there's hope for you.

So go ahead. Experiment with the lessons from this book and see if they don't help you to become a happier and more resilient *you*. Let the inspiration from these pages become a part of who you are, because the strength that each author drew upon comes from a source that's available to you too: the Savior.

You've got this!

HANK SMITH leads off this lineup of authors with a look into the story of Joseph in Egypt. Hank grew up in St. George, Utah, and served a mission in California. He earned an MBA from Utah State University as well as a PhD from Brigham Young University—where he is now a faculty member in the religion department.

Hank, his wife (Sara), and their five children live in Mapleton, Utah. He says, "Sara is incredible. She knows everything about me and still loves me." Hank enjoys running marathons and eating out a lot—which is why he runs marathons.

He has spoken throughout the country for corporations and school assemblies, and he speaks with programs such as The Best of Especially for Youth and Time Out for Women. Hank has published fifteen "Talks on CD" with Deseret Book and Seagull Book. (Please do not drive while listening to Hank's CDs. Studies show that sleeping while driving has a tendency to irritate other drivers. Listen and drive at your own risk!)

SHAPED THROUGH OUR TRIALS

Hank Smith

I am a scripture guy. I've taught from the scriptures as a full-time seminary teacher and a BYU religion professor now for almost two decades. I see the stories, doctrines, and principles in the scriptures as the stuff of the eternities. While I couldn't choose a favorite story or character from the scriptures, certain stories and characters have impacted me more than others. It is these stories that get me bubbling over with excitement when I enter my classroom, and I don't know of many stories that make me more excited and inspired than the story of Joseph of Egypt (see Genesis 37–45).

JOSEPH'S STORY

The first night that Joseph, son of Jacob, slept in an Egyptian prison must have been one of the lowest points in his life. He must have looked up to the stars outside through the bars in his window and thought, *God, why do you hate me?* He must have said, "Every time I have something going for me, you allow someone to take it from me." Through tears, he probably said, "Why is this happening to me?"

Just a decade earlier, Joseph had been a teenager in Canaan. Life was good. His parents, Jacob and Rachel, absolutely adored him. At the time, Joseph was excited for the future. Excited for all the good things his father was telling him were going to come his way. Jacob wasn't the only one telling Joseph about his future. God, through Joseph's dreams, was giving him glimpses of what was going to come.

Then one day, it all changed. It one moment, all that was important to him was taken from him. Joseph's brothers, in an act of jealousy and anger, sold him to a group of Ishmaelites. His brothers turned their back on their despairing brother as he was taken away. Days later, the Ishmaelites sold Joseph as a slave to Potiphar, a member of the Egyptian military.

What Joseph's older brothers did to him was callous and cruel. He did not deserve such horror at the hands of those who were supposed to love him. Joseph should have been able to look to his older siblings for support and guidance, but instead all he received was pain and betrayal. He was now all on his own.

Incredibly, somewhere along the way, Joseph accepted his situation. He wasn't going to get his old life back. Nobody was coming to save him and take him home. If he was going to make something out of this tragedy, it was entirely up to him. Perhaps he said to himself, "I am going to be a slave for a long time. I'll work hard to make something out of this."

Joseph eventually became the "head servant" in Potiphar's house. In fact, Potiphar trusted Joseph so much that he gave him control over his entire estate without ever checking on him. He handed Joseph the Egyptian Bank Account, the Egyptian Express Credit Card, and the keys to the chariot. Potiphar felt lucky to have the best servant on the earth working for him.

If Joseph's story were to stop there, it would be an amazing story. It would be a testimony that betrayal can be overcome, that anyone can succeed despite the pain of other people's choices. Joseph would have showed us that life doesn't have to be defined by the pain others cause through their own selfish decisions.

But Joseph's story wasn't over. He was going to be betrayed again.

Potiphar wasn't the only one who thought highly of Joseph. Potiphar's wife had evil ideas of her own. She tried to coerce Joseph into a sexual relationship. Joseph refused. He had too much respect for Potiphar to hurt him like that. Joseph stayed true to his love for God and the commandments. He told Potiphar's wife he would not commit such a "great wickedness." To make sure he didn't give in to the temptation, he ran away and removed himself from the situation.

Potiphar's wife was likely not used to being turned down. She was embarrassed and angry. She accused Joseph of attacking her. Potiphar was furious with Joseph and sent him to prison. For the second time in his life, everything had been taken from Joseph by the selfish and cruel choices of others.

As he lay in the Egyptian prison, looking up at the heavens outside his window, tears must have been streaming down his face. At this point, he could have easily given in to the anger and hatred. He had every right to be angry. He had every right to hate many people—his brothers, Potiphar's wife, and Potiphar. Perhaps he was angry with his father for not coming for him. Perhaps he was even angry with himself. He may have shaken his head at his own naivety. How could he have allowed himself to trust someone again? How could he have been so foolish to believe that he could have happiness in life? Perhaps he was angry with God for allowing this to happen. Perhaps he doubted that God loved him or even cared about him. Perhaps, in his darkest moments, he doubted that God actually existed at all.

God had a much bigger plan in mind for Joseph, but Joseph didn't know that. All he knew was that he was in an Egyptian prison and may never get out. This may be where he would spend the rest of his life. For all he knew, he was going to die within those walls.

Incredibly, Joseph did the emotionally impossible. Somehow, he found the mental and spiritual strength to reach deep down and decide he could make something out of his horrible circumstances. Perhaps he said to himself, "I am probably going to be here for a very long time. I'll work hard to make something out of this." And just as he had in Potiphar's house, Joseph eventually became the "head prisoner" in the dungeon. The keeper of the guard trusted Joseph so much that he gave him control over all the prisoners without ever checking on him.

If Joseph's story were to stop there, it would be an incredible story. It would be a testimony that not only one, but multiple tragedies can be overcome. It would be an example of perseverance and dedication overpowering the negative effect of others' choices. Once again, Joseph would have shown us that life doesn't have to be defined by the pain others cause through their own self-centered choices.

But Joseph's story wasn't over. In his interaction with the other prisoners, Joseph was introduced to Pharaoh's chief butler. He interpreted the dream of the butler with one request. He asked the butler to "make mention of [him] unto Pharaoh, and bring [him] out of this house [prison]."

After the butler was released, Joseph must have been waiting in anticipation. Surely the butler would do what he said he would. This must be Joseph's big chance. When Pharaoh hears of Joseph's gift, he will surely want Joseph to work for him. The last verse of Genesis chapter 40 is quick for the reader, but must have been a slow and crushing realization for Joseph: "Yet did not the chief butler remember Joseph, but forgat him."

For two more years Joseph sat in prison, forgotten.

But God hadn't forgotten Joseph. Through all of the ups and downs of Joseph's life, God had been moving him into a specific location. But it wasn't only geography that mattered. Not only did Joseph need to be in the right place at the right time, but he had to be the right kind of person when he got there. Joseph's trials were shaping him for this future. Without the difficulties, God could have put Joseph in the right location, but Joseph would not have been the type of man he needed to be in order to become what God intended him to become. In order to do what he needed to do next, Joseph needed to be in Egypt, but he also needed to be wise. It was what Joseph had been through that had given him wisdom: the wisdom that only comes from experience. It was wrestling with the effects of betrayal; it was the experience he gained working in Potiphar's house; it was the years in prison. Through it all Joseph had changed, he had been schooled and shaped through both prosperity and suffering. And now he was finally ready.

In a single day, Joseph's life had been seemingly ruined by his brothers many years previous. But now, in a single day, his life would to change dramatically for the better.

Joseph likely woke up that morning and assumed it would be like any other. That all changed when word came that Joseph had been summoned out of the prison. By who? The pharaoh himself.

Pharaoh had been suffering from the same dream night after night. A dream he didn't understand. His butler then remembered a young man from the prison, a young man that could interpret dreams. So Pharaoh sent for Joseph.

Joseph interpreted Pharaoh's dream and laid out a plan to save Egypt from an upcoming seven-year famine. Because of this, in a single day, Joseph went from being a prisoner to second-in-command in Egypt. From prisoner to Vice Pharaoh. Quite a promotion.

If Joseph's story were to stop there, it would still be an extraordinary story. It would be a testimony that God keeps his promises. The promises He made to Joseph in his early life were being fulfilled in God's own time. He had shown Joseph his incredible future and it was unfolding before Joseph's eyes. Joseph showed us that our trials can be gateways to future happiness and prosperity.

But Joseph's story wasn't over. Joseph was about to see his brothers again.

The famine Joseph saw in Pharaoh's dream became a harsh reality, not only for Egypt, but for all the neighboring lands. Joseph's father and brothers, still in Canaan, were also suffering. They heard about the food stored in Egypt, and Jacob sent ten of his sons to Egypt to buy food.

For Joseph, that day must have begun as any other. He was now married and had two sons, Ephraim and Manasseh. The days of being a slave and his time in prison were distant memories. Life was, once again, happy. Perhaps he was in the middle of a friendly conversation or conducting official business when he noticed a large group approaching. Perhaps there was a first glance, then a turn to take a second look. Then the recognition must have swept over him. His mouth probably dropped open a little, his heartbeat probably quickened. He likely couldn't stop staring. *Is it really them? What are they doing here?*

This was where Joseph was going to find out what the decades apart had done to him and to them. What kind of man had he become? What kind of men had they become?

Joseph decided to test them.

Joseph disguised his voice and spoke to his brothers through an interpreter. He accused them of being spies for the enemies of Egypt. In response, they told Joseph who they were and where they were from. They explained that they were from a family with twelve sons—the youngest, Benjamin, was back in Canaan with their father, and that the other was dead. They had no idea that their dead brother was standing in front of them.

Joseph replied that he would believe them if they could produce their younger brother. One brother, Simeon, would stay in Egypt in prison. The rest would go home and return with the younger brother. With Joseph listening on, the brothers spoke to one another about the past, the pain they still felt over what they did to him so long ago, and how they were still suffering from what they had done. Joseph learned that they had also suffered all these years.

Hearing their regret, Joseph had to leave the room. He exited and wept.

The brothers returned to Egypt from Canaan with Benjamin. Joseph released Simeon from prison and arranged a feast for him and his brothers. After a wonderful evening, Joseph told them they would return to Canaan with their sacks full of food. He told his guards to sneak a silver cup in Benjamin's sack.

Not long after the brothers began their journey back to Canaan, Joseph's guards caught up to them and accused them of stealing from Joseph. The sacks were opened and the silver cup was discovered. They returned to Egypt where Joseph told them that Benjamin would be executed, but the rest could return home.

Would they walk away from Benjamin like they walked away from him all those years ago?

The brothers, with Judah as their spokesman, offered themselves in the place of Benjamin. They couldn't return to their father without him. They had broken their father's heart once and wouldn't do it again.

What must have the brothers been thinking when this Egyptian ruler sent his guards away so he could be alone with them. Tears were flowing from his eyes. They must have wondered, *What is going on? Why is he doing this?*

Then, in a mere sentence, their lives changed forever.

"I am Joseph; doth my father yet live?"

The shock of this statement came in waves. First, they were surprised he spoke their language. He had mentioned Joseph, their brother. Had they ever said his name to this man? Then recognition flowed, he doesn't just know Joseph's name. He had said, "I am Joseph."

Joseph realized they were stunned. They didn't comprehend what he had just said. He saw that they needed a closer look. A small smile came across his lips as he said, "Come near to me. I am Joseph your brother, whom ye sold into Egypt."

It was as if they had seen a ghost. They whispered his name in near disbelief and gathered around him. Joseph embraced each of them, one by one. Tears of joy pooled, then dropped from all of their eyes.

As the shock wore off, there was a realization of what needed to be said. They needed to tell him how they had suffered for what they did to him. They needed to tell him how sorry they were. They needed to tell him how they had wished every day since they last saw him that they could take back what they had done. His anguished face as the Ishmaelites carried him away had never left them. His screams for help had haunted them. They had never had a truly happy moment since that day.

Joseph saw the regret in their eyes. He knew what they wanted to tell him. He put his hand up to speak to them. He had thought through exactly what he would say at this moment. He needed to ease the pain in their hearts. He said slowly and quietly, "Now therefore be not grieved, nor angry with yourselves, that ye sold me hither: for God did send me before you to preserve life." This was God's plan for Joseph. He was where God wanted him to be. He had never truly been alone.

ETERNAL PRINCIPLES

The story of Joseph of Egypt is one of the greatest stories ever told. I believe that heaven designed that story to be preserved in order for us to find comfort and peace in what we learn from the details. In my own personal study, I have found myriad principles in Joseph's story that have brought me profound solace during the most difficult times of my life.

God can use the damaging choices of others to lead us to where He wants us to be.

The Lord frequently reminds us that he can make "all things" work together for "our good." This includes the choices of others. When Lehi spoke to his son Jacob, he reminded him of the difficult childhood he had because of Laman and Lemuel, and then told him God would "consecrate [his] afflictions for [his] gain" (2 Nephi 2:2). When Joseph Smith was incarcerated in the deplorable conditions of Liberty Jail, the Lord told him, "all these things shall give thee experience, and shall be for thy good" (D&C 122:7). Heavenly Father isn't caught off guard by the cruel choices of others. On the contrary, His infinite foreknowledge enables Him to use those choices as tools to shape us into what He'd have us become.

One example is Karl G. Maeser. I've often been amused by how Karl G. Maeser, the founding principal of Brigham Young University, first came to hear of Mormonism. In the early 1850s, Maeser was teaching in the Budich Institute in Dresden, Germany. While there, he came across an anti-Mormon book written by Moritz Busch. Maeser and his brother-in-law Edward decided to investigate this new religion further. Soon, both he and Edward and their families joined the Church. We should all be thankful to Moritz Busch for writing that book!

Often the most difficult times in our lives pave the way to future happiness.

Speaking on having patience through difficulties and trials, President Dieter F. Uchtdorf taught, "Often the deep valleys of our present will be understood only by looking back on them from the mountains of future experience. Often we can't see the Lord's hand in our lives until long after trials have passed. Often the most difficult times of our lives are essential building blocks that form the foundation of our character and pave the way to future opportunity, understanding, and happiness."[1] If you are in the middle of terrible difficulty, perhaps now isn't the time to try and understand God's purposes for them. Concentrate on moving forward through this low valley toward the mountains in front of you where you'll be able to look back and understand.

Some of the greatest men and women ever born found opportunity because of the hard times they went through. Had Joseph never been sold by his brothers, he never would have interpreted Pharaoh's dream. Had Alma the Younger never been spit on in Ammonihah, he never would have met Amulek, one of his dearest friends. Had Esther not lost both her parents, she never would have been able to save her people. Had Joseph Smith's family not lost all of their crops to freezes in Vermont, they never would have moved to New York where Moroni had buried the plates. Perhaps this great difficulty you are going through is leading you to something you will love.

God uses trials to shape us into the type of people we have to be in order to fully enjoy the future opportunities He has prepared for us.

Elder Richard G. Scott, who passed through heartbreaking trials himself, taught, "To exercise faith is to trust that the Lord knows what He is doing . . . for your eternal good even though you cannot understand how He can possibly do it. . . . Your Father in Heaven and His Beloved Son love you perfectly.

They would not require you to experience a moment more of difficulty than is absolutely needed for your personal benefit."[2] It is crucial to remember that your "personal benefit" is at the heart of your trials and difficulties. This knowledge doesn't take away the pain and heartache, but it does give it purpose. Elder Scott was able to touch lives through the decades of his ministry, in part, because of what he had suffered.

My friend and fellow author, Kris Belcher, wrote of the difficulties she's had over her forty years of life in her book *Hard Times and Holy Places*. After cancer took a great deal of her vision as a child, the cancer returned again in her adult years and caused her to go completely blind. Her advice to her readers was to not "allow your heart to be hardened by hard times; make the choice to turn to Christ. There is a purpose in your suffering. You and I are being changed, remodeled, stretched, and polished for eternal glory. If we trust in and choose Christ amid our difficulties, our hard times will become holy."[3] Though Kris has lost her sight, she says, "My vision has never been clearer." She now travels the country as a speaker, changing lives with her humor and enthusiasm.

The trials you are going through now may be the key to you having the knowledge you need in order to become effective in your career, understand your future child's or spouse's mental illness, or save a family member from poor decisions. The circumstances will vary with as many people as there are on the earth, but the Lord's strategy is still the same. He uses our trials to change and prepare us to be successful in future opportunities.

The impulses of the natural man can have devastating effects on our own lives and on the lives of those we love.

Joseph's brothers and Potiphar's wife can teach us about the damaging effects that come from allowing the natural man or woman to control our decisions. We often don't need the Lord to send us trials because we do too good of a job creating our own. This mortal life has enough trials built into it; we shouldn't be making decisions that we know will add trouble it. Because the brothers lashed out in anger against Joseph, they not only ruined Joseph's life, but stole happiness from their parents, and ruined what could have been years of happiness for themselves. The decisions of the natural man leave a bad aftertaste. For Joseph's brothers, it was a bitter aftertaste that lasted decades.

Because Potiphar's wife allowed lust to cloud her thinking, Joseph's life was destroyed and the entire household lost the benefit of having Joseph to manage the estate. Potiphar must have had his doubts about her story. Joseph was always honest with him and had never acted in such a way before. What must have that doubt done to their marriage? The natural man sacrifices long-term goals, which are truly important, for short-term satisfaction and painful consequences. A fool's bargain!

Be smart. Christ calls us His disciples because he expects us to be disciplined!

Forgiveness is an essential virtue in becoming what God hopes for you to become.

Joseph's story could have ended much differently had he allowed anger to fill his heart. When he saw his brothers again he could have exacted revenge and put them into slavery or sent them to prison. As second only to Pharaoh, he could have done the same to Potiphar's wife. He could have had the "satisfaction" of watching them all suffer. But why didn't he? Elder James E. Faust taught, "If we can find forgiveness in our hearts for those who have caused us hurt and injury, we will rise to a higher level of self-esteem and well-being. . . . Only as we rid ourselves of hatred and bitterness can the Lord put comfort into our hearts."[4] Joseph understood that forgiving those who hurt him was a gift for himself. He understood that their suffering would not heal the wounds they had inflicted upon him. Hatred and revenge would keep his wounds open, but the Savior could heal them completely.

Can you can see why I get so excited about the story of Joseph? His story isn't just about him; it's a story about all of us. It's a story about how God works in the lives of His children. It contains principles that guide and heal. Joseph's story is one of the greatest ever told because he allowed the Lord to tutor him through his trials.

NOTES

1. Dieter F. Uchtdorf, "Continue in Patience," *Ensign*, May 2010.
2. Richard G. Scott, "Trust in the Lord," *Ensign*, November 1995.
3. Kristin Warner Belcher, *Hard Times and Holy Places* (Salt Lake City: Deseret Book, 2009), 23.
4. James E. Faust, "The Healing Power of Forgiveness, *Ensign*, May 2007.

WHITNEY WILCOX LAYCOCK grew up in Provo, Utah (except for several childhood years spent in New Zealand and Chile). She served her mission in Málaga, Spain—the same mission where her older brother had served five years earlier. In 2015, she graduated from Brigham Young University with a degree in communications and a minor in sociology. Currently, she is pursuing her master's degree in English at Weber State University, where she also teaches undergraduate writing classes. She met her husband, Landon, at her missionary homecoming. They have been married for two years and are currently living in Lehi, Utah.

BRAD WILCOX, Whitney's father, shares some insights after his daughter's chapter. He also grew up in Provo (except for childhood years spent in Ethiopia). He served his mission in Chile and later returned to serve as a mission president. He is a professor at BYU and has served as a member of the Sunday School general board. Together, they make one impressive daughter-father duo.

HOME

Whitney Wilcox Laycock

There were no spiked gates guarding the houses, no men coming up to wash our car windows at intersections, and no yellow buses zipping through the city streets. Even though Utah was where I had lived most of my life, everything seemed foreign to me when I returned after spending three years in Santiago, Chile. I became even more aware of the differences a week later when I entered tenth grade at Provo High School.

It was strange attending a predominantly white school again. I had spent the previous three years in an international school in Santiago where classes were a hodgepodge of students from China, India, Russia, and many other countries. I guess Provo High wasn't all white—it was about 50 percent Latino at the time I attended, and something about passing the Latinos in the hall and hearing them speak Spanish made me feel more at home, but it didn't make up for how uncomfortable the transition was. Everything was different, even the cafeteria food.

My family had just returned from Chile, where my dad had been called to preside over the Chile Santiago East Mission. Except for those three years in Chile, and a semester in New Zealand where my dad conducted a study abroad for Brigham Young University, I had lived in the same house my entire life.

It surprised me then, after returning to Utah, that I felt more like an outsider in my native country than I ever had in Chile. In Chile, I was the only blonde among a sea of black hair. I could not have looked more different. Back in Utah with my old group of friends, I fit in physically, but on the inside I could not have felt more different. The girls I had called friends now wanted to talk only about boys, clothes, and cell phones—things that had not been important to me in Chile. *It's not supposed to be this way*, I thought. *I'm home. I'm supposed to feel happy.* But inside, I felt miserable and longed to return to my adopted country.

A few days after school started, I met with a counselor at Provo High to modify my school schedule. We talked briefly about how my adjustment was coming along.

"How are you feeling being back at school in the States?" she asked, grinning.

"Fine. It's different."

"I'm sure. I bet you are so happy to be back with your friends."

On the outside, I smiled my plastic smile, the one I had given every day for a week since returning to Utah. I didn't tell her that for the past few days I had eaten lunch in a closed bathroom stall. I wasn't happy to be back with my friends. I didn't know them anymore. I didn't *want* to know them anymore. They hadn't lived in Chile and been through what I had, and I didn't particularly care to explain it to them. None of my friends knew what it was like to visit members of our Church who lived in homes with dirt floors and no roofs, but I did. None of them knew what it was like driving in the biggest car on the street and seeing little children without shoes run up to sell us a box of Band-Aids, trying to earn a few pesos. None of them had ever experienced Chile—a country where some people lived in cardboard houses, where buses honked endlessly, and where three-legged dogs roamed the dusty streets looking for a place to die. Where women left their gated homes and went to the market every morning for freshly baked bread, passing the man in neon blue sweats performing his morning aerobics to "Ring My Bell," the disco beat blasting out his portable boom box. A country where the sunset was a fiery orange every night, where people you didn't know kissed your cheek, and where hope for many came in the form of a cheap box of cigarettes.

Of course, when my parents first told my younger brother, David, and me about the move to Chile, we were not very excited. It took us a few months to warm up to the idea. I already felt awkward enough as a thirteen-year-old battling braces. The idea of living in a foreign country where I couldn't even speak the language made me feel hopelessly out of place. When we arrived in Chile, everything was different from what we were used to. The food, the language, and the culture were all new. For a few weeks, David and I backed away when the Chilean people would lean in to kiss us on the cheek. We didn't realize what they were doing was typical of a Chilean greeting. During those first few homesick months in Chile, I longed to return to Utah and my friends and I fantasized about the day I would be with them again. I seriously doubted whether I would even be able to handle spending the next three years in Chile, much less learn to love it and consider it home.

I vividly remember my first few weeks in our new home. We arrived in Chile in June 2003. It was wintertime, and the dismal weather seemed to fit my mood. On our second Saturday there, our ward hosted a picnic to welcome my family. My parents were gracious recipients of their displays of affection, but my brother and I sat down on a wooden bench somewhat apart from the rest, creating a barrier between us and them. David and I commiserated about how we must be the only kids who ever had to move to a foreign country. In our wallowing, we didn't notice a stocky girl break apart from the group and come up behind us. Without a word, she took David's hand and placed a thick breaded sausage into it. Into mine, she put something resembling a doughy meat pie.

We looked up to identify the person who had invaded our space. Like others we had met, she had mid-length brown hair and her cheeks were dotted with freckles, but her dark eyes were unlike others we had seen. They were softer, somehow, and rich, like warm maple syrup. She was a few years older than I was, and when she smiled, her eyes crinkled and her face reflected genuine kindness. David and I vaguely recognized her from church the previous Sunday, and were pretty sure her name was Mirna.

"Choripan," she said, pointing to David's hand.

"Cherry-pan," we mimicked.

Mirna smiled. "Empanada," she mouthed, gesturing to what I was holding.

"Im-pen-a-da."

She spent the rest of the afternoon with us, teaching us the Spanish words for *tree*, *grass*, and *sky*, and we taught her how to say those same words in English. (It's funny how two cultures can look at the same objects and label them so differently.) Mirna thought she was giving us our first Spanish lesson, but in reality she was breaking down the barrier that David and I had created.

Along with teaching us new vocabulary, Mirna also introduced us to the rest of the *jovenes*, or youth, in the congregation. It wasn't long before we joined them in gunnysack races and learned the proper way to spin tops. Any attempt at conversation made by either side usually ended in confused laughter, but like toddlers playing, we didn't need words to understand what our hearts communicated. I didn't realize it at the time, but that day was monumental because it marked the beginning of my immersion into a new culture, the time when I began to view the world differently. It is also when David and I began to develop a deeper bond of friendship.

Not all my early snapshots of Chile are as happy. David and I started our new school a couple weeks after arriving and we did not receive as warm a welcome there as we had at the church picnic. Because it was an international school, all grades (K–12) met on the same campus. That meant that even though David was in sixth grade and I was in seventh, we could still meet up for breaks and lunch. It also meant that everyone—teachers, students, and staff—spoke and communicated in English. However, even knowing the language didn't stop me from feeling nervous on my first day. I remember one of my teachers asking me to introduce myself. Her question was simple enough, one the other students were used to, but to me it seemed like the thousand-dollar question on *Jeopardy!*

"So, what does your dad do that brought you to Chile?"

Most answered that their father was a diplomat, an ambassador, or a businessman. For many of the students in the international school, moving had become second nature. How did I explain that we had just left everything for the next three years—home, friends, school, even my dad's old job—because leaders in our Church asked us to?

"Whitney?"

"Um, well, you know the missionaries you see out on the street? Young men in suits and ties? My dad is in charge of them."

Blank stares. A mixture of confusion and pity spread across my classmates' faces. Even the teacher seemed surprised.

"In all of Chile?"

"No, just in a part of Santiago."

"And so does he travel a lot?"

"Actually, we aren't allowed outside the boundaries of the mission."

"So you have to spend three years in a part of Santiago?" a girl starting to experiment with blue eye shadow chimed in. "Like you're under house arrest? I thought my dad's job was bad." The class roared.

A few days later, I was climbing up the staircase to get to gym. Two Chilean boys, Fernando and Juan Carlos, came up behind me.

"Hey, new girl!" Juan Carlos shouted.

I closed my eyes. Should I just keep climbing and act like I didn't hear? I cocked my head back to look at them.

"Fernando thinks you have a nice rear end."

Only he didn't say *rear end*, but instead used a term that I had never heard in reference to me before. I turned around and ran the rest of the way up the stairs. I moved quicker than normal as I entered the female changing room and assumed my usual spot in one of the bathroom stalls. This time, instead of changing, I sat on the toilet seat and choked back sobs as I waited for the last cluster of girls to leave before I could bury my head and cry.

Just a few months ago, my dad had promised that this would be a good experience. Sitting in those stiff airplane seats, I had dabbed my puffy, red eyes with the warm towels the flight attendants brought. My dad had put his arm around me and squeezed my hand three times. *I love you*, my family's silent code.

"This will be a good home for us, Whitney," he whispered. "I promise."

Being sworn at was more than I had bargained for, however. I felt that my dad had lied to me. When school finally ended and our driver took us home, I dashed up the white cobblestone, past my mom's extended arms, and hurled myself onto my bed. There, buried under a foot of pillows, I cried until my nose got stuffy.

"Whitney, do you want to tell me what's wrong?"

My mom stood at the door. Through my tears, I recounted the story, embarrassed to tell her what was actually said.

"I hate it here, Mom. Do you know what one of the girls said to me the other day? She said we were under house arrest. Mom, this is like a prison. Why did we have to move? I just want to go home and be with my friends."

She didn't say anything, but instead she sat next to me and stroked my hair until my eyes closed. I don't know what my mom said to my dad, but I do know that David walked with me to gym class for the next month. My old self would have been annoyed at being followed around by my eleven-year-old little brother, but this was my new life.

I had never paid much attention to David before we moved. Other than the occasional fight, we had pretty separate agendas. In Chile, however, he became my best friend. Because we had no one else, we took the time to get to know each other in a new light.

David first earned my respect when, about three months after arriving in our new home, we coaxed the two sister missionaries staying with us to play a game of hide-and-go-seek tag. Our parents were away at a training, which meant that David and I had free reign of the house and the afternoon. As one of the missionaries rounded a corner, about to grab my sleeve, I jerked away, and the hand that would have tagged me struck out and knocked off a porcelain statue of Don Quixote. It fell to the floor, decapitated. Never one to be unnerved, and anxious to resume the game, David rushed to locate a ping-pong ball, which he decorated with a Sharpie smiley face and placed on top of the statue's hollow neck. I'm pretty sure it stayed there until my parents discovered it a month later.

David and I spent most of those three years in Chile together. We soon gave up trying to make friends at school because most of our classmates couldn't understand the odd boy and girl from Utah and left us alone. Whenever our classmates did engage us in conversation, it usually centered around our beliefs.

"So, why don't you wear tank tops like the other girls?" I remember Noelia asking me this on a particularly warm Santiago day as we walked to gym class.

"My Church asks us to be modest and wear sleeves."

"But why do they care?"

I thought about it for a long time. Growing up in the Church I had always simply obeyed. There were things you did do and things you didn't do; I had never stopped to think about the reasons.

"I guess they just want people to respect us for what's inside, not what's outside."

Noelia seemed satisfied and didn't press the issue.

Other times the inquiries came from teachers and staff. I remember taking a glove to class one day to teach my classmates how we viewed the relationship between our spirits and our bodies. I explained that our body is like a glove covering our spirit; it looks like our spirit but when we die, we leave our bodies behind temporarily. Because of Jesus, I explained, we would all be resurrected and have physical bodies forever. Another time, I was asked to prove the existence of God. In order to do so, I brought a copy of the Book of Mormon to class and read the promise found in Moroni. I then explained how each person could pray and ask for himself or herself if God was there.

Between being asked questions at school and being surrounded by the missionaries, I began to do things I had never done at home. I really read and studied the Book of Mormon, my prayers became more sincere, and I started taking notes during General Conference sessions. Not only was I experiencing the world in a new light, I began to view the Church differently as well. Being away from my friends in Utah helped me open up and get to know new people and appreciate different ways of life. Defending the Church helped me understand the reasons behind what we do. My experiences in Chile shaped and defined my values. Before I knew it, three years had passed and it was time to leave.

During our last week in Chile, our ward came together like they had to welcome us, but this time it was to say good-bye. With moistened eyes, Mirna approached me and we spoke together in fluent Spanish. She handed me a farewell gift—a beautiful book about Chile. It was one written for tourists, with an inscription on the front page that read, "When the gods created the earth, they gathered the best parts from every continent and put it all together in one spot they called *Chile*." There were grandiose pictures of volcanoes, lakes, and fjords in the South, places I had never seen because I was under "house arrest" in Santiago. I still have that book, but it does not represent *my* Chile. My Chile wasn't volcanoes; it was the nutty, roasted smell of the caramelized nuts sold by vendors on street corners. My Chile wasn't lakes; it was the feeling of rough whiskers against my cheek when a man gave me a *besito*. My Chile wasn't fjords; it was Mirna, David, and me, and the tears we cried when we said good-bye. Sometimes my Chile had tasted bitter, like the olives in the empanadas, but it also tasted sweet, like *manjar* in the pastries. My Chile is the home I never intended to have, but the one I needed.

Life changed again after returning to Utah. It was hard coming back because Utah was no longer my only home. My friends in Utah didn't understand what my Chile was like; they only saw what was in the tourist book. Many of them were members of the Church, but some were not living the way they were supposed to. The only people who understood what I felt and what I had been through were my parents and David. But my parents were pulled in a thousand different directions almost the moment we landed. My dad had to start back at his old job, my mom was excited to reconnect with extended family, and even David changed. We were older—I was sixteen and David was fourteen when we returned—and we were expected to act like it. I'd felt free in Chile, free to befriend a sibling, free to discuss the Church, free to spend lunchtime how I wanted, and free to be different. Back with my old friends, I felt the need to conform, to refit into a peer group that had carved me out.

It's been ten years now since we returned to Utah from Chile, and I'm finally beginning to understand why that time meant so much to me. My dad hadn't lied to me all those years ago on the airplane; Chile had been a good home for us. But home is more than four walls and a roof, or even what country you are living in, or where you came from. Home is the experiences you have and the people who make you who you are. I am a product of many different homes, and will have many more homes in my future.

I hadn't planned to move to Chile. Our experiences are not always ones we plan. Many times, however, those experiences are what make us who we are. Change is hard, but it's change that allows us to constantly learn and grow, that gives us empathy, and that fills us with hope. While hiding out in the bathroom stall at Provo High, I wanted to return to Chile. Then I realized that all I had learned prepared me for that moment. I realized I was building walls again, just as I had done in Chile with Mirna, only this time, the wall was between my old friends and me. This time, I didn't have Mirna and David to help me break down those barriers.

Soon I broke through one wall—literally—by deciding to stop eating lunch in the bathroom stall. Slowly I began to adjust by making the proactive decision to put others before myself. Rather than focusing on the differences between my old friends and me, I tried to find similarities. When they invited me to hang out with them, sometimes I took pictures of Chile to show them, so that they could understand a little more about what those three years had been like for me.

Just because I had moved didn't mean I had to abandon who I had become in Chile. I might not have been surrounded by as many nonmembers in Utah, but I realized I could still bring up the Church in conversations with my friends. Perhaps I was not able to spend as much time around missionaries, but I could still keep up good gospel study habits and be an example to others. Likewise, maybe David and I were not able to spend as much time together as we had in Chile, but I determined that I had faced tough transitions before, and had made it through.

I realized I couldn't live in the past, with my childhood adventures, an international school, and the Santiago sunsets, but understanding the past was a way for me to move forward with my future. Just as I had in Chile, I would find my place and be better for it.

THE CHALLENGE OF MOVING

Brad Wilcox

Whitney has written beautifully about dealing with the challenge of moving. It is a struggle that many have faced and—though not easy—it can push us out of our comfort zones in positive ways.

When I was a child I remember our family moving to Ethiopia, Africa, where my father and other professors worked to improve the quality of education. My earliest childhood memories are all of Africa, so when we moved back to the United States, when I was almost eight, I experienced culture shock. My mom told me I came home crying after my first day of school, and when she asked me what was wrong, I responded, "Mom, everyone is white!"

Similarly, my wife's family moved often when she was growing up because her father was in the Air Force. They moved from Colorado Springs to Tokyo, Japan, when Debi was in high school. She claims she was sheltered from most of the trauma associated with moving because she had her brothers and sisters around her—especially her twin brother who always acted as her built-in friend. As their father, I'm grateful that's the role Whitney and David played for each other in Chile.

But what happens when you don't have a brother or sister to fill that role? As I consider the moves that have disrupted my life, both as a child and as an adult, I have always been thankful for the Church. How blessed Latter-day Saints are to have a supportive community and network of friends wherever we go.

Most religious people face quite a challenge when they move. They sever ties with their former congregations and must begin searching for a new spiritual home. They often go from church to church and pastor to pastor for months until they find one where they fit best. Latter-day Saints don't usually do that. We just look up the location of the nearest chapel, find out when the meetings are, and show up. Within minutes, people are recommending doctors and dentists and telling us which teachers to avoid in the local schools.

When I served as a mission president in Chile there was a twenty-three-year-old convert who received a visa to go to New Zealand to study English. It seemed like a great opportunity for this young man so I pulled him aside after a meeting to find out more about his plans. I asked, "Who is picking you up at the airport?" He said, "No one." I asked if he had a place to live, if he spoke any English yet, and if he had any money. He answered no to every question. I quickly called a bishop in Auckland, New Zealand—Anthony Wilson—and explained the situation. In true Kiwi form, Bishop Wilson said, "No worries!" He assured me that he and his family would meet the young man and make sure he got settled. They were willing to take this young man in without even meeting him or speaking his language, simply because he had been baptized a few weeks earlier.

This example of sincere friendship and fellowship is not uncommon in the Church. Sometimes we are the ones welcoming others and sometimes we are the ones being welcomed. Either way, membership in the Church is a blessing. Of course, I'm well aware that there are some who take advantage of the quick trust and willingness to share that members offer so freely. We have to be wise and careful, but that doesn't change the fact that Latter-day Saints can make moving just a little bit easier and more bearable for each other.

I'm grateful that my life has been blessed and enriched by members of the Church who have been like an instant family wherever I have gone. As a child living in Africa, I attended worship services in people's homes and primary classes in my friends' bedrooms and kitchens. As an adult, I moved my family to Wyoming, where I was pursuing my doctorate at the university in Laramie. I will forever be thankful for members there who helped us find a home to rent and welcomed us into their circle. The friendships we made there have lasted throughout our lives. I served my first mission in Chile, so going back as a mission president was joyful to me, but it was difficult for my children. What would I have done without the young LDS Chilean girl who welcomed Whitney and David so lovingly? I didn't know Mirna before we moved to Chile, but I prayed that someone would be there to reach out to my children. Mirna was an answer to that prayer.

Christ moved when he was a child. He spent childhood years in Egypt, a foreign land. He later moved to Nazareth—home for his parents, but not for him. He must have experienced being the new kid without many friends. Despite the difficulties that must have presented, He "increased in wisdom and stature, and in favour with God and man" (Luke 2:52). We can strive to do the same wherever we happen to be, and we will be better for it.

We can discover what Whitney discovered—that "home is more than four walls and a roof, or even what country you are living in, or where you came from. Home is the experiences you have and the people who make you who you are." Like Whitney, we are all products of many different homes—including a heavenly home from which we have all moved away and to which we can all hope to return.

DALLAS LLOYD is from Lindon, Utah, and graduated from Pleasant Grove High School in 2010. Chile has played an important role in Dallas's life (just as it did for the authors of the previous chapter) because he served his mission there. Dallas currently lives with his wife, Libby, in Palo Alto, California. He received his undergraduate degree from Stanford in science, technology & society with a concentration in innovation, technology & organizations. Currently, he's working on completing a one-year masters program in the Department of Communication. He's excited to play his fifth, and final, year for the Stanford football team. Upon finishing the season, he plans to chase his dreams and prepare for the NFL Draft.

Dallas enjoys the beach, playing the piano and ukulele, reading books (especially in hammocks), attending his wife's musicals and plays, and hiking. He loves living an active lifestyle and playing competitive games like spike ball, can jam, beach volleyball, golf, pickle ball, and tennis.

TAKE THE ROPE
Dallas Lloyd

lick. Clack. Click. Clack. Click. Clack. Our cleats tap the cement floor as we approach the light at the end of the tunnel. It's dark in the tunnel, though. My hands begin to shake. I close my eyes, take a deep breath, and say a prayer in my heart. Suddenly, my senses heighten, and time freezes. Chills run up and down my spine. The roar of 95,000 fans nearly deafens me. A B-2 bomber flies overhead. This is the Rose Bowl—The Granddaddy of Them All! A record 28.2 million people are watching the game on television. *Is this really happening? Am I really starting as safety for Stanford? About to play in the Rose Bowl?* What was merely a childhood dream had somehow become a reality. Four years earlier, when I returned from my mission to Chile, I could have never imagined the journey that would lead me to this moment.

As I sat in an interview with my mission president the day before my return to the United States, he asked, "Elder Lloyd, are you still planning on attending Stanford and playing football there?"

"Yeah, I'm so excited to get started. I'm nervous, though," I said, thinking of how hard school and football would be.

He took a deep breath and started in, "Elder, your testimony will be tested. Your burdens will be heavy. The adversary will try to lead you astray, and temptations will be overwhelming."

I nodded in agreement. I knew it would be hard to stand alone in my faith.

President Gillespie looked me straight in the eyes and said, "No, Elder, he will place every roadblock he can in front of you to keep you from what God has in store. But like you've learned here in Chile, if you remain faithful, the Lord will be with you, and will guide you every step of the way. You'll have the opportunity to impact and bless so many people."

When my plane departed for the United States, a piece of my heart was left behind with the Chileans. It will always belong to them.

Upon returning home, I trained extensively for three months to prepare myself for the rigors of collegiate football. Physically, I needed to gain the strength, speed, and weight that I had lost on my mission. Spiritually, there was no greater preparation I could've done than serve a mission. I felt ready to dominate the Stanford football scene. As the top quarterback recruit in Utah history up to that point, I was excited to contribute to the success of Stanford's offense. Mid-June, I packed up my belongings and drove out to Silicon Valley—

leaving behind the safety net of family and religion that I had grown up with.

At six o'clock a.m., the alarm clock blared letting me know it was time for "intellectual brutality" as they call it here at Stanford. My roommate (also a new freshman) smacked the snooze button, while dropping his usual curse word or two. We were both dreading the workout ahead of us. Every morning was the same routine preparing for these grueling workouts. We would wake up, chug a full twenty-four-ounce Gatorade, and scarf down a banana. Failing to nourish our bodies before the workout could result in us passing out. Workouts consisted of two parts: first, running and conditioning on the field; and second, lifting in the weight room. Doing planks on our elbows, football-field-length bear crawls, eternal wall sits, and shuttle runs (wearing weight vests) in what felt like Olympic-worthy times were a few of the training methods they used on us freshmen.

Each workout was designed to make us question our mental and physical capacity to finish the task. Our muscles would be far past their breaking points, and yet we would still hold a pushup position. The mind can make the body do anything. Even though our muscles were cramping and screaming at us to quit, the weight of our success as a team depended on our individual ability to persevere and push aside the physical pain. Each day, I was mentally and physically exhausted.

One particular morning workout was the hardest of them all: Take the Rope. The upperclassmen had warned us about this day, and now it was here. I walked into the weight room after completing a strenuous run. The upperclassmen were waiting with four forty-foot ropes. They were thick and rough, reminding me of ropes used to dock a boat. Our strength and conditioning coach gathered us around. After a whole summer of demeaning remarks and tough love, now his instructions seemed to be encouraging us. In that moment, I knew this would possibly be one of the hardest physical experiences I would ever encounter. He explained the rules of Take the Rope.

"It's basically tug-of-war: One of you against twenty of the upperclassmen. You will never physically be able to take the rope from them. They will slowly give it to you at their discretion."

All of us looked at each other, not sure how this would turn out.

He went on. "Rule number one, don't drop the rope. Two, keep pulling—hand over hand. There's no resting. Three, your feet must stay behind the line." He looked with confidence into our eyes. "Four, never give up."

I was the second freshman to take the rope. After watching my friend struggle with the rope for ten minutes, he finally finished pale-faced, eyes dilated, and looking as if he'd seen a ghost. I was terrified. Shaking, I picked up the rope. Immediately, I was whipped across the line.

"Get behind the line!"

Determined, I planted my feet firmly behind the line, bent my knees, and began to pull hand over hand.

The upperclassmen bombarded me with ruthless phrases and endless vulgarity:

"You suck!"

"Just drop and this can all be over!"

"We don't need you!"

"Mommy's not here to help you now!"

"Look me in the eyes!"

"Go back to Utah!"

I lost all sense of time. My vision started to blur, and all the sounds around me became a muffled hum. My teammates shook the rope violently, causing the flesh on my fingertips to tear. They threw it on the ground and stood on top of it, making it impossible for me to pull. I became so fatigued that I began to doubt I'd be able to finish. In that moment, my coach's instructions became my escape path: *hand over hand*. Focusing on one hand movement at a time allowed me to concentrate on the progress I was making, rather than the pain I was feeling. I grunted with each tug as I incoherently mumbled to myself, "Hand over hand. Hand over hand." When I finally pulled my last teammate across the line, the whole group immediately circled around me, showering me with praise. One of them brought me a Gatorade and as I tried to grab the bottle, I realized my hands were bloody and I couldn't keep a grip on it. Clearly knowing my struggle, he poured it into my mouth. Mentally and physically this was new territory, a new sense of accomplishment. Although the workouts continued to be seemingly unbearable, I could look back on that moment and draw strength.

The challenges seemed endless as I struggled through the physical and mental battles of workouts, and learned one of the most complex offenses in the nation as an incoming quarterback. And spiritually, I was facing a battle I'd never fought.

On a team of one hundred, I was the one and only Mormon. It was an experience unlike anything else. People were curious. Some had never met a Mormon, while others hadn't even heard of Mormonism. Questions such as, "How many wives do you want to have someday?" "What does it mean to be Mormon?" "Why don't you drink alcohol?" "Why are you still a virgin?" and "Why did you live in Chile for two years?" were asked daily. I loved the opportunity to share my beliefs and introduce them to my faith. In the classroom setting, it was refreshing to experience such political, cultural, and religious diversity. I enjoyed having my own voice and a different perspective, while simultaneously learning from and listening to my peers' various viewpoints. However, this was not always a positive experience. More often than not, I was required to stand up for what I believed to be right.

During the fall of my freshman year, there was a lot of buzz about the presidential election between Barack Obama and Mitt Romney. One day at lunch, I grabbed the usual grilled chicken, brown rice, and spinach and sat down at a circular table with my friends. The table just to the right of us drew the attention of the room with their loud conversation. A tall kid with blond curly hair and glasses seemed to be the ringleader. He kept generalizing the Republican Party in a negative way and bad-mouthing Mitt Romney. I thought, *Whatever. He's entitled to his own opinion. He's just sharing his own political views.* But then his negative words shifted specifically toward Mormons. His face grew redder and redder, and his tone of voice grew in conviction and passion as he spouted off facts that he claimed were true about Mormons.

"Mormons will do anything to become rich, especially if that means neglecting poor people and being dishonest. That's how Mitt Romney got all his money." At this point, my friends had stopped talking and were all looking at me.

"Did you guys know that Mormons dig up dead people from their graves and baptize them?" His peers gasped. The emotions in me started boiling. I was upset that this guy who knew nothing about my religion was acting as if he knew every little detail. It took him a mere two minutes to destroy everyone's view of Mormonism, while I had dedicated two years to teaching people about it. He continued, "Mormons believe that war is always the answer and that killing people is encouraged to solve problems." I couldn't take it any longer. With my friends staring at me, I mumbled, "That's it," and stood up and walked over to him.

"Excuse me," I demanded his attention. The whole table looked at me.

"You don't know what you're talking about. I'm Mormon and every single thing you've just said about Mormons is false. If you don't like Mitt Romney, then don't vote for him."

He looked at me with a smug little smile, "Oh, was I wrong? Please enlighten me."

I knew his intentions were not to actually learn and have a discussion, but to start an argument. So I looked him in the eyes and said, "You might want to do your research before you teach others about something you know nothing about." I grabbed my half-eaten lunch, threw it away, and marched out of the dining hall.

Just as my mission president said, I was forced to share my testimony in many instances where it could've been easy to back away. But I was eager to receive the blessings from staying faithful that he had promised. I was working hard at both my faith and football.

Despite my greatest efforts, things on the football field weren't working out. The quarterback one year ahead of me in school had solidified his position as the starter, and the coaches had given me a small role. I had a small section of the playbook with plays designed specifically for me. I saw action in most of our games my sophomore year, and even had a run for twenty yards against the University of Utah at Rice-Eccles Stadium. Despite some cool experiences, I was frustrated with the little amount of playing time I was receiving, especially since I'd been working so hard in the weight room, film room, and on the practice field. Where were the blessings? In a game at the end of my sophomore year, we were beating Cal by forty points and my coaches still didn't put me in. *This is unbelievable*, I thought.

One day, I'd had enough. I walked into my head coach's office and asked if he had a few minutes to talk with me. He shut the door and asked, "What's going on?" After telling him my frustrations, we had a long and meaningful conversation about how I could potentially help the team by switching from quarterback to safety. We agreed that the position change would be a long, hard road, but that it would be for the best. The next day at practice, I ran with the safeties. The drills felt foreign to me. Backpedaling? *I haven't backpedaled in seven years*, I thought. The playbook I had worked so hard to learn became useless, and it felt like I was learning Spanish all over again.

At that point, I felt as if I'd reached the bottom. I was frustrated with the life-ruining choices people were making all around me. I was back to square one with football. In my classes, my beliefs were considered naive, and even my professors challenged what I thought to be true daily.

I'd reached a critical crossroad: I could either give up, feel bad for myself, and succumb to the lifestyle of those around me; or I could continue with faith, pressing forward. Coincidentally, it was at this time that I met Libby. I was home visiting family, and mutual friends set us up on a date. After that initial date, our dating was entirely long distance. We would read scriptures together over the phone and have many deep conversations about the gospel. This helped me refocus on the scriptures as a source of strength and guidance. Along with consistent study of the Book of Mormon, morning and evening prayers became my favorite part of the day. My mentality started to change.

I felt as if I was in the middle of my own "Take the Rope" challenge, only with different stakes. In the workout, my teammates had shaken and stood on the rope and insulted me with the intention of making me fail. Quitting seemed to be the only pathway to relief. In my life, my peers' obsession with alcohol, girls, and parties weighed me down. I couldn't escape the temptations that surrounded me. Hand over hand, I prayed for my friends and served them, even when that meant keeping them safe by being the designated driver. Hand over hand, I shared the gospel when it wasn't the popular thing to do. Hand over hand, I focused on the small things that I could control, like reading my scriptures and saying my prayers. I saw these situations as challenges from Heavenly Father to prove myself and learn from the experience. Remembering that Heavenly Father simply wanted me to try, and that to keep going was a key factor in my success. For Him and through Him, I could hold on to the rope and "never give up."

As soon as I had this shift in perspective, the blessings of heaven came pouring down. I was able to maneuver through challenges with confidence. My relationship with Libby blossomed and we were married in the Salt Lake Temple. Instead of worrying about myself, I began to spend my time focusing on others. Happiness came easily.

Switching positions and working to excel as a defensive back was no longer a trial to endure; it was an opportunity to chase my dreams. The Lord placed two very special people in my path: Richard Sherman and John Lynch, two of the best defensive backs in the history of football.

In his first years at Stanford, Richard Sherman played receiver and was moved to defensive back. Now he's considered the best defensive back in the NFL and was recently featured on the cover of the football video game, Madden 15. I met him a couple months after the Seattle Seahawks's Super Bowl victory. He was wearing gold boots, a chain, sunglasses, and a cool Seahawks hat. *This guy is the man. He was the hero of the Super Bowl*, I thought as I sheepishly approached him.

John Lynch was a quarterback at Stanford and was moved to safety. He eventually became a Pro Bowler (the NFL version of All-Star) and candidate for the Pro Football Hall of Fame. Lynch came back to Stanford in order to finish his degree, and we happened to be in the same business class. We were even assigned to the same group for our group projects. The timing of these encounters was impeccable and I knew that the Lord was looking out for me.

On separate occasions, both Sherman and Lynch rejoiced upon hearing about my transition from offense to defense. They both encouraged me to transfer all of the knowledge I'd gained as a quarterback to the way I play defense. Shortly thereafter, I looked for ways to follow their counsel and apply my offensive knowledge to defense. I was able to understand and manipulate quarterbacks, depending on the situation they were in. After all, I used to be a quarterback. This intellectual, yet physical game of cat and mouse excited me. My ability to outsmart offenses and predict plays proved to set me apart as a defensive back. I eventually excelled and won the starting job. Fall of 2015 was my first year as a starter, and the season was one for the record books. We were dominating. We had a great season with the most wins in Stanford football history, beating USC twice, Notre Dame, and UCLA. We finished the season ranked #3 in the country.

Bang! Bang! Confetti cannons fire and the crowd erupts. My body is sore and weak, but my mind is racing. My teammates and I embrace and tears of joy fill our eyes. "We did it! We won the Rose Bowl!" Clouds of red and white confetti fill the brisk Southern California air as the television cameras surround us. Standing on the podium as they present the Rose Bowl trophy, I reflect on my journey up to this point. A scripture comes to mind:

> For verily I say unto you, blessed is he that keepeth my commandments, whether in life or in death; and he that is faithful in tribulation, the reward of the same is greater in the kingdom of heaven.
>
> Ye cannot behold with your natural eyes, for the present time, the design of your God concerning those things which shall come hereafter, and the glory which shall follow after much tribulation.
>
> For after much tribulation come the blessings. Wherefore the day cometh that ye shall be crowned with much glory; the hour is not yet, but is nigh at hand. (D&C 58:2–4)

ZANDRA VRANES is an author, speaker, and social media producer. She believes that humor and faith can go hand in hand. (Watch how she takes the story of Joseph in Egypt, which we explored in the first chapter, and turns it into something completely different with her trademark flash and wit.) Zandra enjoys cowriting sistasinzion.com (a humorous, faith-based lifestyle blog) with her partner in crime, Tamu Smith. The duo also coauthored the hilarious and inspiring book, *Diary of Two Mad Black Mormons: Finding the Lord's Lessons in Everyday Life*. Zandra lives in Boise with her hubs and their pet Chihuahua. In kindergarten, she told everyone at her school that her mother had died. Her mother is still very much alive and reminds her of her lie on a regular basis.

GOD'S GOT YOUR BACK

Zandra Vranes

L ife sucks, then you die." I had a friend in high school who had this phrase on a T-shirt; she wore it all the time. You know those people who think depression is a fashion statement, not a medical condition? That was Jess. If she had a spirit animal, it would probably be Eeyore, the gloomy donkey from Winnie the Pooh. She was always saying things like, "I'd rather be crying than smiling 'cause tears are like anchors that sink your heart to the bottom of the ocean floor." Um, what? Or, "Did you know that guys prefer girls who are melancholy?" I don't know what teen magazine she was getting her stats from, but the majority of the high school boys we knew couldn't spell "melancholy," let alone want a girlfriend who was.

While Jess's shirt, which declared that life stinks right up till the end, might resonate with us when we are going through trials, thank goodness it isn't true. Now don't get me wrong, I know life ain't all fun and games. We all go through struggles, and hardships, but in between "life is so messed up" and "RIP" there's a whole lot. There's joy, growth, change, happiness, contentment, and much, much more. The world wants us to believe that where we are right now is as good as it gets, and if where we are right now isn't so great, the devil wants us to think that we can only go down from here. But the devil is a lie, y'all! 2 Nephi 2:25 tells us that "Men are, that they might have joy." You hear that? God wants us to be happy; He didn't put us on this earth just to endure the journey, but to also enjoy it. Rely on the Lord, for only He can turn a mess into a message, a test into a testimony, a trial into a triumph, and what's broken into something beautiful.

Sometimes when life gets you down it's hard to talk about it. I should know. I'm the queen of keeping everything bottled up inside 'cause I don't like folks all up in my business. Privacy is important, and when others share personal matters with us, we shouldn't be running off and sharing it with Tom, Dick, Harry, and Twitter. There's nothing worse than confiding in a friend and then finding out that they made your personal drama their Facebook status. However, I'm learning that keeping it all in isn't always the right answer, and as I continue to allow Heavenly Father to direct me, He puts me in the path of people who I can open up to. We also keep things inside when we think that sharing it with someone else will result in embarrassment. I get it; I've been embarrassed more times than I care to count, and I don't know why so many of those experiences involve an LDS chapel and a man named Mr. Lee.

Mr. Lee was a family friend who often accompanied my grandmother when she attended church with my family. He was a retired school bus driver with a mouth full of dentures who spoke like his jaw was full of bubble gum, only it wasn't. No one could ever understand what Mr. Lee was saying, unless what he was about to say was going to be so embarrassing that you prayed the earth would open up and swallow you whole. Of course, in those moments, Mr. Lee made an exception and spoke exceptionally clear.

Mr. Lee was also a Bible-thumpin', foot-stompin', Southern Baptist. He liked to shout enthusiastic "Amens" and "Hallelujahs" to confused LDS sacrament meeting speakers. This didn't faze my siblings and me; in fact, we often coaxed him into a few 'cause it made church so much more fun. But on this particular Sunday, oh boy! Mr. Lee took it to a whole new level. During the passing of the sacrament, the time when the chapel is most silent, Mr. Lee grabbed the wrist of the deacon, who had just finished passing us the water and loudly proclaimed, "Them lil' altar boys done drunk all the wine and filled these cups with water!" Oh my goodness! I wanted to die and be resurrected in a time when Mr. Lee had all his teeth, but never, ever opened his mouth. And why was he looking at us with that triumphant grin on his face, as if he had just solved a crime? In my head, I was screaming, "Sit down! You are not a detective and this is not CSI!"

My parents quickly and quietly tried to explain to a disbelieving Mr. Lee that the "altar boys" were actually deacons who had not in fact drunk any wine, and that the cups were always intended to be filled with water. As the deacon who was trying desperately to hold back his laughter collected the tray, I thought to myself, *I will never live this down*. I remember taking that long walk of shame to my Sunday School class after sacrament meeting was over and praying that maybe somehow everyone had forgotten about Mr. Lee's outburst during the beginning of the meeting. Oh no they hadn't, and it was all everyone was talking about. My face burned with embarrassment throughout the rest of the church services.

There are experiences I had as a child that absolutely mortified me, but now I can look back at them and laugh. This is one of them. Today I would give anything for my grandmother and Mr. Lee to visit church with me and bring their upbeat praise and worship with them. Now that they have both gone on to be with the Lord, these are fond memories that I cherish. Sometimes the further we get from a situation and the more life we experience, the more we can realize that circumstances that seem embarrassing can teach us and even bring us joy. So don't be embarrassed to talk with the right person about what's got you down.

The right person to talk to could be a friend, a parent, a counselor, a youth leader, or even the bishop. I remember the first time I needed to talk to my bishop about a situation as a youth. I worked myself into such a frenzy that I couldn't eat, I couldn't sleep, and I couldn't concentrate on anything other than worrying about what I needed to talk to the bishop about. Prior to that, the bishop's office was a happy place where I could go get candy after church. Now that I needed something other than candy, it kind of felt like the principal's office. I was sitting in the foyer outside the bishop's office, sweating as if I'd stolen something, and was on the verge of vomiting when he finally called me in. I didn't know if I was supposed to sit or stand, or if he was going to make me place my hand on a Bible and swear me in, like what I'd seen on *Judge Judy*. The bishop offered me a seat and began to talk to me. It was nothing like the principal's office . . . not that I'd been there a lot . . . Eventually, I nervously told my bishop the reason for my visit. He listened. He didn't scream and yell, he just listened, and when I had it all out, he counseled with me.

Today I know that the bishop is not "the punisher." His role is one of love, and if we have strayed, he can help us get back on the path that leads to our Savior. We shouldn't be afraid to seek our bishop's guidance, and we don't have to wait until we are seeking repentance to see him. Shoot, I'm up in the bishop's office all the time now. I still go there for the candy, sometimes I go for priesthood blessings, and other times I talk to him about situations in which I was the victim. It's important to remember that the Atonement of Jesus Christ is not just for being forgiven, but it can also help us to forgive others, or to feel peace when someone else has stolen it from us. Elder Timothy J. Dyches said, "If you feel unclean, unloved, unhappy, unworthy, or unwhole, remember 'all that is unfair about life can be made right through the Atonement of Jesus Christ.'"[1]

One of the fastest ways to forget to look up to God is by looking around at what you think everybody else has got. We always think that the kid around the block has it so much better than we do, and maybe they do, but coveting what they have isn't going to make us happy; it's actually quite the buzzkill. When I was a youth, I was always comparing my life to others, and it's a hard habit to break. I used to look at the images in church magazines and think, *My family looks nothing like this.* In the *Ensign*, you see these well-dressed families gathered for family home evening and the kids are all sitting still and listening and the parents are smiling and there's a yummy plate of treats. *Puh-leeze*, FHE at my house was always a hot mess! Somebody was always crying, nobody was listening, my parents were yelling, and someone inevitably got a whoopin'. I just wanted God to make my life "normal." As I started to really study the scriptures, I learned that my life wasn't as abnormal as I thought it was. I'm serious. Have you really taken a close look at the people in the scriptures? First of all, the scriptures are better than any reality TV show; there are families in the scriptures that make Honey Boo Boo and her crew look completely sane.

Take Joseph in Genesis for example; this dude's life was not anything that would be considered "normal." To start with, he was born out of this crazy love triangle. His dad, Jacob, wanted to marry his mom, Rachel, but on the wedding day, Joseph's grandpa (Rachel's dad) pulled a bride switch and Jacob ended up accidentally marrying Leah, Rachel's sister. You see what I'm saying? Who needs Snapchat when there's all this drama in the scriptures? Okay, so now Joseph's daddy is finally able to marry Joseph's mama and they have Joseph. But by the time

Joseph came on the scene, his daddy already had a bunch of other kids. See, this is where I realized that this scripture story was gonna be more similar to my life than the people I was always trying to compare myself to. 'Cause in my family, there are nine kids and three baby mamas, and as we can see from Joseph's family tree, a blended family is not a new concept.

Like some of us, Joseph was born into a family that had a long history of drama. His mother and the aunt that his daddy had accidentally married didn't get along. He had two brothers, Simeon and Levi, who were duckin' the popo 'cause they had killed all the people who were responsible for the assault on their sister Dinah. Y'all, and this ain't even the half of all that was going on. So his family is under some stress, and to make matters worse Joseph's daddy declares that Joseph is his favorite child. You might be thinking, *Well that's not so bad. All parents have a favorite child, even though they try to act as if they don't.* No, Joseph's daddy was not just acting as if he had a favorite child—he gave Joseph a special robe to wear so that not only could Joseph know he was the favorite, but everyone else could know too. You can imagine that this didn't make Joseph very popular, and added a whole lot of drama to a house already full of it. Also, his daddy, formerly known as Jacob, changes his name to Israel. (Now this might be confusing to a lot of people, but for those of us with folks in our family who have aliases, we know what time it is.) Things got harder for Joseph, because his mother, while giving birth to his younger brother Benjamin, passes away. So here he is, a very unpopular teenager in a dysfunctional family, and his mother dies. It had to be hard.

Now this is where Joseph and I start to differ a lil'. Joseph is a snitch. When he and his brothers are out working in the fields, he runs back and tells his daddy all the stuff that his brothers are doing that they aren't supposed to be doing. To top it all off, Joseph starts having dreams about how his brothers will one day bow down before him . . . *and then tells his brothers about the dreams!* Who does that? In this regard, Joseph was not the sharpest tool in the shed. Look, you can't have all that baby mama drama in the house, be the favorite, walk around in an outfit that screams, "I'm my daddy's favorite," tell your older siblings you 'bout to be the boss, and be a snitch. Where I come from, snitches get stitches and end up in ditches, and that's exactly what happened to Joseph. Some of his brothers decide that Joseph is trippin' and that they're gonna kill him and throw his body in a pit. I already told you that there were some ex-cons in the family, so don't act shocked. His older brother Reuben, who has a lot more sense, says, "Let's not kill him. Let's just throw him in the pit." So that's what they do. Reuben's plan was to rescue Joseph from the pit later that day, but while he was gone, the other brothers ditched the pit plan. Upon seeing a caravan of merchants roll through town, they decide to sell Joseph to the merchants and then stage his death. So they pull him out of the hole, sell Joseph into slavery, take his fancy "I'm so special" robe, smear it with goat's blood, take it back to their father, and tell him that Joseph, his favorite son, is dead. This was before CSI, DNA evidence, and all that, so Jacob totally buys the goat-blood story and is devastated.

So, a lot is going on in Joseph's life: he's a slave in Egypt, and all he was trying to do was get through puberty. Po' baby! Joseph, throughout all these trials, kept his eyes on the Lord. But his focus on the Lord didn't mean that Joseph's struggles came to an end. After being sold, he ends up as a servant in a house owned by a man named Potiphar. Joseph works hard and earns all kinds of promotions, and just when it looks like things might be looking up, he ends up in prison for a crime he didn't commit. But staying close to the Lord strengthened his faith, and he knew that God would help him overcome the very hard obstacles life had thrown his way.

Like a lot of people I know, Joseph found Jesus in jail. When I was younger, I used to ear-hustle on grown folks' business (okay, so I was nosy, but I still wasn't a snitch) and I'd hear them talking about someone who just got done doing time and they'd say, "You know, she made some real bad mistakes, but praise the Lord, she found Jesus in jail and gave her life over to God. Now we gotta keep her in prayer and hope she chooses to stay on the straight and narrow." I would think, *I wonder why we go to church all the time? Apparently Jesus is stayin' over at the jail, 'cause everybody is finding him there.* Of course, now I understand that Jesus is at church and he's at jail, because the Savior doesn't leave us when we're down, and no matter how low we've sunk, we can always choose to turn around and return to Him.

That's how it was with Joseph. He was locked up, but God had not forgotten him. Through a series of events inspired by the Lord, Joseph was freed from jail. He was promoted to a high station, this time in the house of the Pharaoh of Egypt. It was a huge deal—like coming out of prison and getting a job at the White House. Meanwhile, back home where Joseph's family was, there's a famine going on; everyone is starving, there's no McDonald's and no dollar menu—I'm talking major hunger here. So Jacob, Joseph's daddy, told his sons, "I hear there's food in Egypt. Y'all should go over there and check it out." So Joseph's brothers went to Egypt to buy food, and guess who's in charge of selling the food? Yep, Joseph! Now Joseph recognized them, but they didn't recognize Joseph. It had been a long time; when they sold him, he was still a teen. Now, his voice had probably stopped cracking and had gotten deeper, and he had started wearing deodorant and stuff like that— he was grown, y'all. What would you do? I've thought about this so many times and I hope that I could be as righteous and loving as Joseph was. Joseph fed his brothers, but more importantly he *forgave* them.

That's the thing about recognizing that God has brought you through a trial. When you know where you've been and you know who's seen you through it, you don't need to hold on to all that hurt and anger. That doesn't mean that you have to kick it with the person who hurt you, it just means you're not going to allow that situation to rule your life. You're choosing to give it over to God. Sometimes you just gotta let go and let

God. Like Maya Angelou said, "Forgiveness is the greatest gift you can give yourself."[2]

One of the greatest tools that we have for looking up in the face of adversity is the scriptures. Just as we go to people in our lives for advice, we can go to our Heavenly Father too. Hold your scriptures in your hand and take a look at them; they are the word of God. If you've ever wished after you prayed that God would just start talking back to you, then you should read the scriptures. They're literally His words! The scriptures contain a whole lot of advice. I know I've shared plenty of advice with you, and you may even have found some of it helpful, but I'm just a resource. God is *the* source. At the end of the day, it's about you and your God. Don't let anything come between that relationship. Elder Carl B. Cook said, "Try not to look sideways to see how others are viewing our lives but . . . look up to see how Heavenly Father sees us."[3]

They say life is a test. Seriously, who likes tests? In school there's sometimes nothing more stressful than a test. All that cramming and studying and note-taking. Here's the thing about tests though. A teacher doesn't administer a test until they have taught you the material that they are about to test you on. So, if life is a test and God is our teacher, then we're in pretty good hands, right? When I'm going through something really hard, I can't stand it when someone says to me, "God never gives you more than you can handle." I know they mean well, and I know that they are trying to encourage me, but sometimes it's discouraging to think that the thing that's got you down, the thing that you're struggling with—you're supposed to be able to handle it. What if we're not handling it, what if we're at our wits' end—does that mean we're a failure?

"But God is faithful, who will not suffer you to be tempted above that ye are able; but will with the temptation also make a way to escape, that ye may be able to bear it" (1 Corinthians 10:13). What if what we mean by "God won't give you more than you can handle" is that God won't let us be tested without providing the education that will allow us to pass? 'Cause why would we get a test that we don't have a chance at passing? Why would God test us and not provide study material? Yes, life is a test, but if we let Him, God will tutor us. So, when life gets you down, don't forget to look up and remember God's got your back!

Hallelujah Holla Back,
Zandra

NOTES

1. Timothy J. Dyches, "Wilt Thou Be Made Whole?" *Ensign*, November 2013.
2. "Maya Angelou: Forgiveness is the Answer," interview by Anja Crowder, ABC News, November 24, 2013.
3. Carl B. Cook, "Look Up," *Ensign*, January 2012.

TAMU SMITH, the other half of the Sistas in Zion duo, is a freelance writer and the coauthor of *Diary of Two Mad Black Mormons: Finding the Lord's Lessons in Everyday Life.* While she enjoys participating in the type of tongue-in-cheek humor found on her website (sistasinzion.com), she finds true fulfillment in looking beyond the surface and finding the Lord's lessons in everyday life. Tamu is known as a busy bee; she finds a way to squeeze every second out of every hour out of every day. She has been cast in television roles and has participated in local and national plays. Tamu wrote an editorial for *Wasatch Women's Magazine,* and she serves on several committees in Provo, Utah, where she resides with her husband and children.

FESS UP TO
THE MESS UP

Tamu Smith

recently told my young adult daughter, "If it doesn't kill
you, it'll make you stronger." As soon as I shared this little
pearl of wisdom with her, I cringed. I had truly become my
maternal grandmother, my Big-Mama. When it came to the
hard stuff, Big-Mama could pull a cliché out of the air as fast
as a magician could pull a rabbit out of a hat. It wasn't the first
time I'd caught myself "parenting thru cliché"—something
I swore I wouldn't do when I was younger. It was, however,
the first time I recognized that my daughter needed more. She
needed more depth, more truth, and more validation. She was
going through one of life's painful transitions, and as much as
I wanted to, I couldn't just place a bandage over these scrapes
to hopefully minimize scarring. For starters, her scrape wasn't a
scrape; it was more of a deep wound. Deep wounds sometimes
require stitches; need to be aired out; or on occasion, need to
be packed daily with medical gauze, cleaned, and repacked. In

any case, most deep wounds don't heal properly only by being covered up.

I did for my daughter what I wished Big-Mama (my maternal grandmother who raised me) would have done for me when I was growing up. I spoke directly about what my thoughts had been when I was younger, regarding this particular cliché.

"When my Big-Mama used to say things like 'if it doesn't kill you, it will make you stronger,' I always thought, *who was the first person to make that claim and why?* Did Adam give Abel that advice right before he suggested that he go talk to his brother Cain? Was Eve given those words of comfort as she was being escorted out of the Garden of Eden? At what point does a person realize, 'I've been through harder trials before, so this situation ain't nothing!' Does going through more trials make a person stronger? Or, do some people just get more trials because they need to exercise faith in God? Should I pinch myself as I'm going through trials as a reminder that it's not really a trial, it's a workout, and I'm just building spiritual muscle and getting stronger in Christ?"

As I finished my rant, her response was reassuring and an answer to my prayer. She smiled. She didn't laugh; she simply smiled through the tears that ran down her face as she nodded in agreement with what I was saying.

That conversation with my daughter made me reflect on a time when I needed to hear more from Big-Mama. I needed to know that she really understood what I was going through. I'd felt alone. I'd hoped that she could connect with me through more than just another dusty old cliché.

I was in the seventh grade, and we were on Christmas break. My two best friends were at my house and we were bragging about our Christmas loot when my mom let it slip that she had recently been released from the CIW, where she'd been for years. I know that some of y'all are probably thinking, "what's wrong with being released from the CIW?" You seriously don't want to confuse CIW with the CIA. CIW stands for California Institution for Women; the only similarity it has to the CIA is that they both have a relationship with the government. If you are in the CIA, you aid the government. If you are in CIW, you are on government aid; it means you are in prison.

My mother had spent the last three years in the CIW. This may not have been such a shock to the system if I hadn't lied to everyone about what she did for a living and where she was.

They thought she was a nurse in the military serving a "humanitarian mission," because that's what I told them. I came up with that lie after being questioned by kids at school about where my "real" mother was. When I told Big-Mama about their questions, she asked me why I bothered hanging with them "lil' simple kids." (In case y'all are wondering, calling someone "simple" will land you in a fistfight where I came from. It's basically a nice way of saying a person is stupid. Some Christians "bless your heart," while others will "bless your little simple heart." Sometimes Christians can be some of the meanest nice people you'll ever meet.) Determined to protect the truth of where she really was, I decided to turn my mother into a "humanitarian." Chalk it up to watching a lot of *M*A*S*H* as a kid. I'd managed to get away with that lie for years . . . until I didn't. On the day my friends found out that my mother was a criminal and I was a liar, I absolutely thought death would be easier to embrace than having to return to school and face them.

By the time winter break was over and we returned to school, everyone knew my secret. Nobody was interested in why I lied about my mother's whereabouts. They didn't care that the fear of being judged led me to lie. The fact that my mother went to prison for defending herself against an abusive husband didn't matter to them either. They had some hot juicy gossip that they wanted to share regardless of who they would hurt in the process. They were either talking about me and my mama or completely ignoring me. When we got back to school, I was notified by one of the girls I ate lunch with that I could no longer sit at their table. She also claimed the other kids were uncomfortable sitting with a liar. As if that wasn't hurtful enough, she told me the reason that my best friends didn't tell me themselves was because they were afraid I might shank them. (When my mother had decided to leave her relationship, she and my stepfather started fighting and she stabbed him. She pled guilty and was sent to prison for attempted murder.) So, it was especially hurtful knowing that the kids were saying I was going to "shank" one of them. She took being a "mean girl" to another level. I wanted someone who could share my burden.

I finally broke down and told my Big-Mama what was going on at school. To this she proudly said, "You go back to that school and tell those kids 'sticks and stones can break my bones, but your words will never hurt me!'" Um, that's not what I wanted to hear from her. Her old-school advice didn't make me feel better; it actually made me cry. That was the same advice she had given me in elementary school! By the time I was in the fifth grade, kids were over that phrase; they had moved on to threatening and cussing. This situation was beyond Big-Mama's ability to handle. I wanted Big-Mama to be as mad at my friends as I was. She could have told me a story about how she could relate because something similar happened to her when she was my age. I wanted her to give me hope or at least permission to cuss the kids out who had been tormenting me. Instead I got a dusty old nursery rhyme and a lecture about lying. Then, as if it were a blessing, she said, "You know the Bible says, 'If it doesn't kill you, it will make you stronger!'" (Whenever Big-Mama wanted us to believe something without question, she would say "the Bible says" . . . even if the Bible didn't say it.) She went on to say, "Maybe God is getting you ready for something. Maybe He's try'na reveal who your real friends are. Look around, who's sticking with you through this? It's probably the "lil' nerdy kid," someone you thought you'd never be friends with." She laughed and then said, "Life is like that."

Not my life, I thought. Big-Mama told me to look for the blessing in this. I didn't have the heart or courage to tell my Big-Mama that her saying was outdated and I was too old to be repeating stuff like that. I needed some original sayings. And just because I wasn't being hit by sticks or stones, didn't mean I wasn't being hit. Words were not only hitting me, they were beating me down. "Look around," Big-Mama said! That was the problem; I had been looking around. There wasn't one kid at my school that wanted to be my friend, not even one of the "lil' nerdy kids." The nerds were way too smart to get caught up with the lying daughter of an ex-convict.

The realization that Big-Mama couldn't walk me through this trial left me feeling even more hopeless. How long would I have to carry the shame of my mother's actions? Prior to joining The Church of Jesus Christ of Latter-day Saints, I belonged to the Church of God in Christ (COGIC). It was there that I learned to have a personal relationship with God and Jesus. My pastor was always saying things like, "When you are going through trials, give Jesus a try." As I looked at the interactions of all the kids at school, I longed to have just one friend. I wished for someone who knew my story and still wanted to know me. I searched for the one "nerdy kid" that my Big-Mama was convinced wanted to be my friend. The more I scanned the hall, the madder I got! Y'all, I did not meet the gaze of one person that wanted to be my friend! To these kids I represented drama, and don't nobody invite drama into their lives unless they are controlling the channel and volume. I can't lie; I halfheartedly hoped that Big-Mama was right, that someone was watching and waiting for me to see them so that we could be friends. When it didn't happen, I was sad. Thinking about the words of my pastor brought the words of a spiritual we used to sing at church to mind: "Take It to the Lord in Prayer." Y'all might know it as "What a Friend We Have in Jesus."

> What a friend we have in Jesus,
> All our sins and griefs to bear!
> What a privilege to carry
> Everything to God in prayer![1]

Had I carried everything to God in prayer? The thought of taking this to Jesus made me feel stupid. Sometimes when I complained about people not liking me or people talking behind my back, Big-Mama would remind me, "So what? Folks talked about Jesus Christ!" Every time she would downplay my feelings in that way, I wondered, *what if Jesus feels the way Big-Mama does?* Was He sitting on a cloud listening to all of our prayers, rolling his eyes and saying, *"Boo-hoo.* So you and your friends are in a fight? What do you want me to do about it? If they ain't nailing you to a cross, don't bother me with your simple problems. I got more important things to deal with." I was struck by the words of the spiritual. "What a friend we have in Jesus, *all our sins and griefs to bear.*" I did sin, and because of my sin I had some griefs. If Jesus really was willing to bear my troubles, who was I to stop him?

I decided I would try Jesus. When I knelt in prayer that evening, I apologized to God for lying and expressed my desire to be a better daughter, sister, and friend. I didn't know how to give my sins or grief to Jesus, so I did what I imagined King David did after he sinned. I begged God to forgive me. I begged God to take my sins and griefs and give them to

Jesus, since he offered to take them. I knew I was asking for a whole lot already, but I had one more request before ending my prayer: a good friend.

The next day at school, I waited for someone to approach me. I waited for someone to meet my gaze, waited for a friend to extend a kind smile. It didn't happen, and I was devastated! I thought about giving up, but then I thought it might be God testing me to see if I had really repented. What if God didn't send me a friend because he was still mad at me? If God was testing me, I was 'bout to pass it. We've all heard stories about people who gave up just before achieving their dream. I was going to show God that I had not only repented, but that I was worthy of a friend. I prayed the same prayer again, but still nothing happened. This went on for weeks and ended with the same results.

I decided I should probably do more than just pray, so I incorporated scripture study into my repentance process. My thought was that if God saw me studying the scriptures, he would know how serious I was and have mercy on me. Searching the scriptures and reading the stories of deception brought me comfort. I especially liked reading about how God delivered Samson after he had sinned and lived a tumultuous life with Delilah. I knew that if He did it for Samson, He would do it for me too. Y'all, I got so caught up in the Bible stories that I decided to take my Bible to school with me so that I could have something to read during lunch. It wasn't like I was trying to impress anyone. After a few weeks I noticed I felt better; not just better, I felt good. Even though my social situation hadn't changed, I felt content with my life.

At some point it dawned on me that I was no longer praying for God to send me a friend. Instead I was praying for myself, my family, and other people in my life. The more I prayed, the closer I felt to my Savior. As I drew closer to the Savior, I understood just how much God loved me. I realized God loves me for who I am, not in spite of who I am. He sent me a Savior. The Savior, who was perfect, took my sins upon Himself. He was willingly crucified so that I could have a chance at eternal life. Jesus went alone into the Garden of Gethsemane where He said, "My soul is overwhelmed with sorrow to the point of death" (see Mark 14:34). I can't pretend that I can relate to the type of overwhelming sorrow Jesus felt. I can only speak to the type of sorrow that weighed heavily on my soul. It was so overwhelming that there were indeed days when I wondered if death would have been easier to face than my friends. I'd read the story of Jesus's experience in Gethsemane and thought I understood it. It was only when I was going through my own Garden of Gethsemane that I grasped—as much as I humanly could—what Jesus experienced there, and how much he loved us in order to willingly endure it. My Brother. My Savior. My Friend! Not only did Jesus know me, He knew that I was more than a sinner, and He still poured His love into my life. I spent so much time begging God to send me a friend that when He did, I couldn't see it because I was too focused on a "true" friend showing up in human form. However, God never loses focus. He sent his Son to shine unconditional love on me. When I realized what was happening, I had to acknowledge Him out loud. "I see you, Heavenly Father! I see you showing up for me! I see you, Lord! Thank you, Jesus! Thank you!"

When we recognize God pouring grace into our lives, it's difficult to remain sad and gloomy, or at least it was for me. I could not contain my joy! I was no longer willing to allow anyone to define me by something I didn't have any control over. I had spent weeks trying to apologize to my friends for lying to them with the hopes that they would try to understand why. Y'all, the problem is when you know that Jesus will show up for you (in righteousness), you start acting like that annoying kid that runs around the playground tellin' all the other kids, "my big brother is better, bigger, faster, stronger, and more spiritual than yours."

Now prior to my newfound courage, I had tried to talk Big-Mama into transferring me to a new school. However, the new me wasn't about to run away from nothing or nobody! Empowered with the knowledge of who I was and who had my back, the only thing I wanted to start doing was mend what was broken, especially since I was partially responsible for breaking it. The Spirit gives you a different type of confidence; it gives you the type of confidence that will make you walk into the Red Sea, without a life jacket, fully expecting to make it safely to the other side. I know that's what happened to Moses, because that's exactly what happened to me, in a roundabout way. Okay, I didn't exactly part a sea, but I did part the hallway of Roseview Junior High School, which was just as dangerous in my opinion. I decided I was done with this nonsense. I was determined to sit at my old lunch table, with some of the very same kids that I'd been eating lunch with since I was in elementary school. When I took my place at the lunch table, a few of them looked at me strange and wanted to know what I was doing at their table. I told them "I'm 'bout to eat lunch with y'all! You got a problem wit' that?" They looked at each other and then back at me and said "No." I replied, "Cool," and it was over. What? It was over! It was a little weird at first, because we hadn't talked for so long, but it was over.

I'm learning to find wisdom in clichés. I understand that there are going to be times when I will have to dig deep to help loved ones get answers. I must admit that I do find familiar comfort in talking about and sharing clichés from my perspective. After all, what didn't kill me made me stronger. Ultimately my goal is to equip them with the understanding that Jesus will always be there. If they will lay their burdens on the cross, He will willingly bear them. All He asks of us is that we give Him a try.

Hallelujah Holla Back,
Tamu Smith

NOTES

1. Joseph Scriven, "What a Friend We Have in Jesus," *hymnal* *.net*, www.hymnal.net/en/hymn/h/789.

CHAD HYMAS has been called "one of the ten most inspirational people in the world" by the *Wall Street Journal*.

In 2001, at the age of twenty-seven, Chad's life changed in an instant when a two-thousand-pound bale of hay shattered his neck—leaving him a quadriplegic. But Chad's dreams were not paralyzed that day; instead, he became an example of what is possible.

Traveling as many as three hundred thousand miles a year, Chad inspires, motivates, and moves audiences, creating an experience that touches hearts for a lifetime. He is one of the youngest ever to receive the Council of Peers Award for Excellence (CPAE) and to be inducted into the National Speakers Association's prestigious Speaker Hall of Fame. He is also a member of the elite Speakers Roundtable as one of twenty of the world's top speakers.

Chad's speaking career in the areas of leadership, team building, customer service, and mastering change has allowed him to grace the stage of hundreds of professional and civic organizations. Chad is also a best-selling author, president of his own communications company, and a recognized world-class wheelchair athlete.

COME WHAT MAY

Chad Hymas

P inned under two thousand pounds of alfalfa, I am alone in the growing darkness, struggling for breath. The laboring tractor engine spews exhaust fumes into my limited air space through the cracked sides of the crushed exhaust pipe.

I am trapped in the seat of my own tractor. I'd seen the flashing red light on the dashboard while I was operating the forklift, warning me that the hydraulic pressure was low, but I had chosen to pull the lever anyway. Ignoring the light had never been a problem for me before. But this time, the lack of pressure had sent the huge bale rolling backward down from the fork—onto me.

Unable to move or help myself, fear—real fear—begins to overwhelm my thoughts. Fear of death, fear of paralysis, fear of tomorrow.

Fear that I will die.

Fear that I won't.

The giant bale of hay crushes my mouth and nose against the dash. I can barely breathe, but barely is better than not at all. Breathe. Just breathe. I scrape my teeth against my lips to force open a bigger gap. I don't care about the blood. I only care about air. *I want to live.*

Fear and fatigue compete for top billing. Heart-pounding panic takes the lead, then overwhelming sleepiness from carbon monoxide poisoning. Sleep. Irresistible sleep. A place of no pain.

I slip in and out of consciousness.

I must face this fear and pain if I am going to stay with my family. I pray. Somehow, now, it seems easier to breathe. I tense up, start to suffocate, pray again, relax a little, and breathe a little easier. I am getting dizzy. I fade in and out, but counting my breaths helps me stay focused and breathing—and alive.

What can you do when you think you can do nothing? You can do something. Focus on the goal—life. Mind the task at hand—the one thing I can do, the only thing I can do—breathe.

Five. Six. Seven. Eight. Nine. Ten . . . Twenty. Twenty-one. Twenty-two . . . Thirty-three . . . Forty. . . The sun sets. The sky darkens. The desert air chills. I grow weaker.

I pray more fervently that I might be allowed to live. The sound of the struggling tractor engine becomes a distant white noise as I focus on doing what needs to be done. Breathe—just breathe.

I slide in and out of consciousness, groggy from pain medication, unable to fully understand what has happened. I see bright glittering stars in front of me. They are so real, so close. I can reach right out and touch them.

Gradually the painkillers wear off. I become coherent, but can't communicate. I am hungry, but can't eat. A plastic tube snakes down my throat. Other tubes run up my nose, down the back of my throat and into my stomach or run up directly into my arm with a needle. One supplies my body with food, another with liquid.

Wires twist over my face. A machine helps me breathe. I am frightened and in pain—but no pain below my upper chest. That frightens me even more. I feel a burning dry thirst and a constant sense

The tractor and the 2800-pound bale of alfalfa from the accident.

of suffocation. Even with the help of a mechanical respirator, I struggle for each shallow breath.

A "halo brace" holds my head immobile. There is nothing angelic about this halo brace. Four screws have been drilled through my skin and into my skull, two on each side above the ears. The pain is excruciating. The foundation of the brace is a large plastic breastplate lined with sheepskin to keep the plastic from irritating my skin. Steel bars are attached to the breastplate, extend up and over my shoulders, and are fastened to the back. The halo brace is connected to weights that hold my head and neck straight and keep pressure off my spine. It allows me to move nothing but my eyes.

My family is gathered around my bed. My wife, Shondell, is holding my hand. I can't feel it, but I can feel *her*. Mom, Dad, and his wife. They are all with me.

They are ready to hear the worst.

I am not.

Three doctors step into the room. They have assessed my injuries and are ready to report their findings.

The damage to my spine is extensive. Three vertebrae—C3, C4, and C5—are fractured. They had already made a six-inch incision in my neck and inserted a titanium plate. My neck is not paralyzed, and the stitches are beginning to burn. Bone has been removed from my right hip to repair the fractured vertebrae.

They are unsure of the prognosis for my spinal cord. It's obviously traumatized or damaged. It may be severed, or nearly so, and I will likely be in a wheelchair for the rest of my life. Or it could be just kinked and eventually straighten itself out. In that case, I could possibly walk again.

For now, I have lost the use of my legs and all of my stomach muscles, so I can't sit up on my own or have any reasonable semblance of balance. I've lost two of the three major muscles in my chest, but I still have diaphragm control, which is why I can breathe, albeit barely. My ability to cough or sneeze is gone.

What about bladder control? Or bowel control? The muscles that control those functions are useless as well. Why is this important? When quadriplegics and paraplegics are asked what they miss most, is it intimacy? Nope. It's bladder control and bowel control. Who wants to wear diapers?

I have lost all feeling and function in my arms, hands, and fingers. I am officially a quadriplegic—all four limbs permanently or temporarily paralyzed.

My eyes are all I can move. I look at each family member. They try to hide their concern and fear. They are unsuccessful. It is difficult for them to digest such tough information. It is hard not to cry.

———————

There is some good news. If my spinal cord isn't severed, I should regain some important functions. "In that case," the doctors tell me, "you will eventually have use of your wrists."

Big deal. I think to myself.

Well, it *is* a big deal. Anything, when you have nothing, is a big deal. A few weeks later, this prediction comes true. I cannot feel my wrists, but I can move them. (Over the years, this has allowed me significant and important functions. Wrist movement gives me great advantage when putting on my shoes, buttering a roll—writing a book. One simple function, a 1 percent improvement, can create a 1000 percent improvement in my quality of life and ultimate independence.)

The doctors predict I will regain the function of my biceps. A couple of months later, this becomes reality. (This is the only usable muscle group I have in my upper arms. I have no triceps function, but I have perfect shoulders and fairly impressive "guns." The miners I speak to regularly are quite impressed when I flex, and my kids pretend to be scared.)

The doctors tell me that one in three chest muscles works. A wonderful one in three. The muscle that is unaffected is my diaphragm. That one muscle allowed me to count my breaths or, rather, gave me breaths to count during those fifty minutes or so while I was trapped under that bale of hay. It is still the only muscle in my chest that works.

The doctors continue, "You'll be confined to an electric

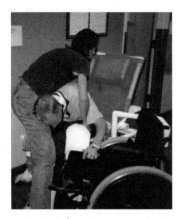

Shondell helping Chad into his chair.

wheelchair. You will learn to operate it by using your wrist or your chin. And one more thing, your body's thermostat does not work anymore. You've lost essential control of body temperature. You have to understand that quadriplegics die easily from heatstroke or hypothermia in circumstances that would merely make others sweat or shiver. You can't shiver—nor can you sweat. You won't be able to enjoy the outdoors the way you have."

Darkness rolls into my soul as evening fog rolls into a darkening valley. I give in to tears. I am hurt, bewildered, and impotent. My soul is in anguish. On top of it all, I am humiliated, because I just can't stop crying.

My response to this news sends my father from the room. He leaves because he knows I am not in a mind-set to be taught. How like our Heavenly Father this is. When we're upset, he doesn't lash out at us; he simply withdraws until we're ready to be taught.

Later on, when my father returns to my hospital room, he asks me, "Will you be teachable?" I'm not sure how to respond, but my father seems to think I'm ready for something more than self-pity. To my surprise, he brings Elder Neal A. Maxwell, a member of the Quorum of the Twelve Apostles, to my bedside.

Elder Maxwell asks me, "What if you could be a better husband and father without the use of your limbs?"

My response still isn't very positive. "I can't be a husband because I can't even hold my wife's hand," I say. "I can't be a farmer. I can't be a hunting guide because I can't ride a horse. I can't be a dad. I can't pitch to my kids or shoot baskets with them." I list several more things that I can't do before Elder Maxwell stops me.

"You're starting all your sentences with the word 'I,'" he says. "The Savior was never focused on himself. And your life isn't about you. Instead of using 'I' so much, use 'you,' 'yours,' and 'us.' This will be of the greatest benefit to people outside this hospital."

Then he goes on to tell me, "You'll need to change some things about yourself."

I'm a little surprised. I thought I'd been doing pretty well. I hadn't been unfaithful to my wife. I'd avoided pornography, and tried my best to make righteous choices.

But Elder Maxwell says, "You're probably going to have to learn to eat differently, court your wife differently, play basketball in a wheelchair, and even read your scriptures differently. How will you dress? You'll need to tie your shoes with your teeth." Then he has me try it, but I protest.

"It feels awkward."

"Disciples of Christ get awkward quick."

I'm not sure that I follow him, but then he says, "If being a disciple of Christ were easy, who would do it? Everyone. If getting married in the temple were easy, who would do it?

Everyone. Only 40 percent do. If being a missionary were comfortable, who would do it? Everyone. Only 30 percent go. You'll need to do things that are awkward. You'll need to learn to do things for yourself, like tying your shoes with your teeth. You'll need to serve without being asked. When your kids are playing ball outside, go outside in your wheelchair to encourage them, instead of staying inside where you're comfortable."

Then this kind man leaves me with something I'll never forget. "What if this could be a better opportunity for you than being a guide ever could? You could be a guide in a different way."

I will later look back on this exchange as something that saved my life.

After sixty-three days in the hospital, I am finally allowed to go home. I realize that my life is not determined by what happens to me, but by how I respond to what happens. It is not about what life brings to me, but rather what I bring to life.

Thoughts are powerful. A change in our thinking changes our lives. Change is not always easy though. Even a change for the better can cause us to feel uncomfortable and unbalanced. Replacing a habit or a belief requires diligent effort. Like anyone going through a traumatic ordeal, I had to make significant changes in order to survive and move forward. Most importantly, I had to change my way of thinking.

Losing the function of most of my body was not acceptable to me. I wanted miraculous improvements—immediately! It didn't happen that way. Getting where I wanted to go was a struggle. Bit by bit, inch by inch, I did the little things: the possible, the achievable. I pushed myself to do the small things, so I could one day get the big things done. And as time went by, a very big thing rose to the top of my list. It was something that thrilled and intimidated me—a goal that I wanted to achieve, both for me and for the people who believed in me.

I wanted to break a world record.

Las Vegas, here I come! After months of training, I was finally ready for a five-hundred-mile marathon. My goal was to beat the three-hundred mile record that my late mentor, Art Berg, had set, by two hundred miles. I wanted to get into the *Guinness World Records*! It would be hot stuff! It would be fun!

Sometimes, my enthusiasm exceeds my reason. But I couldn't see a downside to this plan. *The trip would be easy*, I thought; after all, I'd be sitting down all the way! I decided to make a plan and execute it as if it were a business goal. I kept it simple. I broke the big goal into little goals.

I calculated the distance between Salt Lake City and Las Vegas on my computer.

Chad's arrival in Mesquite, Nevada, at two in the morning. It was one of the final stops in his ultra-marathon between Salt Lake City and Las Vegas.

It didn't take long. Las Vegas was actually 513 miles away. I decided that I would do fifty-three miles each day and arrive at the Mirage Hotel and Casino in Las Vegas in ten days. If I *did* every day what needed to be *done*, I'd get the big thing *done*. 513 miles. A world record.

DAY ONE—JULY 27, 2002

I push off from Salt Lake City's Temple Square at four in the morning in Art Berg's custom three-wheeled cycle. I would sit in my cycle, low to the ground with my feet strapped straight in front of me. My arms would do all the pushing, with pedals just like any other bike.

In six hours, I complete my fifty-three mile goal. I feel great. Why not push farther? So I push an extra twenty-eight miles! My brother Jeremy rides beside me on a bicycle. This is fun.

A hospital visit from Art Berg (right). Art was a quadriplegic, a motivational speaker, and world-class wheelchair athlete. His ultra-marathon record was the one Chad aspired to break.

DAY TWO

There is some uphill and a twenty-eight miles per hour headwind. I have to push hard. I even have to push downhill. This is not so fun. My arms are weary, my neck and shoulders ache. I quickly gain a greater appreciation for Art Berg's three-hundred-mile record. By the end of the day, my hands are blistered and bloodied. The doctors and my wife ask me to stop, before I do permanent damage. I'm not going to reach my goal today. I did twenty-eight extra miles yesterday, so I'm still on schedule. Tomorrow will be easier.

DAY THREE

It isn't easier. I'm in trouble. Headwinds continue. I still have to push my chair downhill. This isn't what I trained for. It is a lot harder than I thought. There are mechanical failures: two flat tires, a broken drive-chain. My back hurts. I didn't know a numb back could hurt. My hands hurt. How can my hands hurt? They're paralyzed. This is not much fun.

DAY FOUR

Beaver Mountain. I've been dreading this. It's a climb of 2,900 feet in just four miles. I am slower than a turtle. I am on wheels, of course, but wheels roll backward too. This is no fun at all. Getting in Guinness doesn't seem so great now.

My father is with me. So is most of my family and a support team. They're trailing me in a nice big motor home, with all sorts of comforts from home. My mom even brought my favorite meals, but I am now too tired to eat.

I pause in utter exhaustion. My wheelchair stops dead as soon as I quit pushing. I have to hold on to keep from rolling back. Dad is beside me in an instant.

"Dad, I can't do this. I can't. I thought I could, but I can't." I say it matter-of-factly. I don't even have the energy to whine. I am tired—beyond tired—and I still have six more days ahead, *if* I stay on schedule. "I am beat. Finished."

Dad says, "Don't think about six more days. Just do one more day. Just for me, son. Just one. If you're really done, I'll understand."

I am too tired to argue.

DAY SIX

I start down the other side of the mountain. Dad is right! Just keep pushing and suddenly things turn your way. Momentum will take over. Momentum is your friend. But that happy thought doesn't last long, as momentum and gravity quickly take me from zero to thirty-nine miles per hour. Thirty-nine miles per hour doesn't seem like much—unless you are only four inches off the pavement. It's pretty scary, but I make up a lot of time. Great! Maybe this *will* work. I feel better. I'll do it one day at a time, like Dad said.

We begin our trek across the Southern Utah desert. Now "one day at a time" is clearly *not* going to work. Asphalt temperatures hover at 122 degrees during the day. It is 120 degrees at two in the afternoon. Silvery images dance off the pavement. I am pretty sure one of those is an angel on silvery wings coming to take me home.

When I decided to get into Guinness, I thought I'd be "hot stuff," but I didn't realize how hot I was really gonna get! I may be numb from my neck down, but the sound of black asphalt sizzling is unnerving.

Ever hear of Mormon crickets? They are huge—big and brown—about the size of overgrown cockroaches. Mormon crickets have a tendency to go on periodic family outings. They must have been planning this trip to coincide with mine, because coincide it did.

We are talking millions of bugs here. They move in waves—mostly crawling, some flying, like an advancing army with spotters in helicopters. They hit that stretch of highway and fry. Miles and miles, millions and millions—*billions*. Layers of dead crickets cover the highway.

I am sitting only four inches above the pavement, which is covered one inch deep with bugs. It is like pushing through pebbles—but I have to keep going. They pop and smell like burning popcorn!

Why did I choose to attempt this marathon in July? Because it is easier for a quadriplegic to cool off than it is to warm up. Ice and a wet towel will do it.

But this heat is too much. There is an executive council meeting in the air-conditioned motor home. We decide I should start working the night shift. Now I wait until 11:00 p.m. to allow the day—and the asphalt—to cool.

"One day at a time" becomes "one night at a time." I push off in the dark, heading toward the light reflected in the sky from the Vegas strip. That heavenly glow becomes my guide. Even from eighty-one miles away, the lights brighten the night sky. It is lovely, but honestly, I am torn up, broken up.

I push two hours on the ninth day. Then everything stops working. My body gives up. Remember, as one who deals with quadriplegia, I don't have any body strength. I have my neck and shoulder muscles and my biceps. That's it. It's like the Vikings trying to push a dragon ship through high seas with the cook and cabin boy at the oars and everyone else asleep in the hold.

The extra miles my ego pushed in the beginning have zapped me and no motivational mantra of, "One day at a time—or one night at a time," is going to get me into Guinness. My wife and my dad offer encouraging words.

"Honey," Shondell says, "how about trying just one *hour* tomorrow? If you can't make it, we can go home." Now it's "one hour at a time"? Whatever happened to "one day at a time"?

Shondell gets me up at six the next morning to try again. She is happy and excited. I am not. She dresses me. I let her. I must conserve every ounce of energy I can.

I push.

One hour.

I collapse.

Instead of counting one day at a time, or even one hour at a time, I am now down to counting mile markers. Reduce big strides into small steps—and keep on going.

But can I really do this? Even one *mile* at a time? I have gone past three mile markers and the next one is nowhere in sight. How do I do ninety more miles? I can't even do one more. I *can't* do this. I am too tired to weep. After 441 miles, a measly 90 miles is going to stop me. Stop me from what? Breaking the world record? No. I beat the world record forty miles ago. This is *my* goal, not anyone else's, and it is tearing me apart that I can't get *done* what I set out to do.

My wife doesn't say anything. Dad steps in, "Son, don't give up. Break down the goal even more. Instead of mile markers, count the yellow stripes in the middle of the road. They come faster. See if that helps."

The next day, I count stripes. It actually works. I do 728 stripes that day.

Every time I feel like giving up on this journey through the desert, I break my goal into smaller increments—one day at a time, one hour at a time, one mile at a time—and now one yellow stripe at a time. In order to survive and succeed,

I have to focus on the simple task at hand and do it. Keep the goal in mind, yes; but keep my eye on the task at hand. It kept me going when I was under a bale of hay—breathe, breathe, breathe. It worked then, and it seems to be working now. Maybe I *can* do this.

Tonight, I sleep the sleep of the Pharaohs—for fourteen long, blissful hours. It is time for one last try. Mind the task at hand. Keep my mind on the goal. Try and try again.

I am pushing uphill. I can't even *see* my goal; Las Vegas— the Jewel of the Desert—beckoning the weary traveler with soft hotel beds, swimming pools . . . All I see is a long, black, hot highway, decorated with yellow stripes, stretching into the distance—uphill.

If I just count the stripes, maybe, maybe, maybe. 758, 759, 760 . . .

Finally, I see the lone, lonely mile marker. I am out of breath. I can't even groan. *Seventeen miles to go.* This is impossible. I have nothing left—nothing. This time, I really don't. I am beyond done. No motivational mantra will move me one more marker.

I reach down into my soul and push painfully. One last push. Personal torture has now become a way of life. I just want to get past stripe 2,763. Suddenly my bike starts rolling on its own.

Wait! Stop it! Don't push! No one can push. That's not allowed. I look behind me numbly. Who is pushing me? No one? An angel?

Nope. I have crested the hill. *It is all downhill from here— all seventeen remaining miles!*

I never thought about that. After going literally as far as I could go, dividing and sub-dividing my goal into smaller and smaller steps until there is nothing left *in me,* Providence steps in. Aching shoulders, blistered and bandaged hands—they don't matter anymore. Providence is pushing me to break the world record.

I coast into Las Vegas on three wheels and a prayer.

They shut down all stoplights on the Strip. Providence keeps pushing. At 9:30 in the morning, with traffic signals stopped and a motorcycle police escort, I coast my way to the Mirage Hotel and Casino. After eleven days, I cross the finish line. It is exactly ten years to the day since Art Berg completed his marathon.

A cheer goes up from thousands of people I have never met. I weep and grin as I realize the value of the lesson just handed me. It's not just about support—with which I was blessed in abundance. It's not just about preparation and planning—which is important. It's not just counting breaths to survive, counting stripes to progress, and doing the small things to get the big thing *done.* It's more than that.

When you decide what you are going to do, and give

Chad entering Las Vegas.

all you've got—really give it all, right down to the soles of your numb and blistered feet—you may get a push from Providence and get all you desire.

You may even get into Guinness.

———————

In his book, *The Impossible Just Takes a Little Longer*, Art Berg wrote, "Life changes. It is the nature of life to do so. For those in this life who choose not to change, life will change for you. And it is always more painful that way."[2] Life has changed for my family and me. However uncomfortable that change may be, it is up to me to decide how to respond.

To regret the experience is to regret the lesson—because the lesson is inextricably contained in the experience. Too often when changes occur and our circumstances are not as we planned, we tend to focus on what we lost, what we've missed, what's gone wrong, who is to blame, and "why me?" We are not accepting the reality of our changed circumstance or the opportunities those changed circumstances present. We ignore the gift of change and delay our progress.

If you are facing a storm in your life—I beg you to determine right now that you *will* look for the positive in every single day. I know there were numerous days while I walked in the "valley of the shadow" that it was difficult not to be consumed by the letdowns and bad news. I also know that our determination to find the positive, no matter how small, played a large role in helping us ride out our storm.

How can we love days that are filled with sorrow? We can't—at least not in the moment. I am not suggesting that we suppress discouragement or deny the reality of pain. I am not suggesting that we smother unpleasant truths beneath a cloak of pretended happiness. But I do believe that the way we react to adversity can be a major factor in how happy and successful we can be in life.

If we approach adversities wisely, our hardest times can be times of greatest growth, which in turn can lead toward times of greatest happiness.

Every life has peaks and shadows and times when it seems that the birds don't sing and bells don't ring. Yet in spite of discouragement and adversity, those who are happiest seem to have a way of learning from difficult times, becoming stronger, wiser, and happier as a result.

Do you ever look at others and wonder how they can be so happy? Everything is going their way and your life isn't that great? I have come up with ten suggestions that will help you have a great attitude and a bright future.

1. Smile

This is the number one rule for a reason. People who smile, even when upset or discouraged, inevitably find reasons to be happy. It takes far fewer muscles to smile than to frown; why waste your energy feeling pessimistic and downtrodden? Putting on a smile is like putting on rose-colored glasses. Give in to laughter, give in to smiling, give in to happiness.

2. Surround yourself with great people

You are only as good as the people you surround yourself with. The people around you have a big impact on you. They impact who you are, how much money you will make, and what you value. They also impact how you think. If you surround yourself with negative people, you will be negative as well. You can't help it. Hearing negativity all day leads you to negativity. The opposite is also true. Surround yourself with positive people, and you will be more positive.

3. Teach

Teach others at all levels as much as you can, as often as you can. Sharing your knowledge with others always makes you feel like you are helping out and serving a purpose. You always have something to share and teach someone else.

4. Be understanding

Understanding is a hallmark characteristic of a powerful young teenager today. Be understanding of others and their situations. We all have bad days. You never know what someone else is going through and dealing with.

5. Delegate appropriately

Don't feel like you need to take on the world and do everything on your own. Ask for help from your friends, teachers, parents, and siblings. More than likely, they are just waiting for you to ask. You would be surprised how many people love to help a loved one.

6. Serve

Find someone that is in need of something and go do it. There is no greater joy than that of service. Mow the lawn for your dad, or do the dishes for your mom. Go visit your grandma, or call up a friend that you haven't talked to in a while. Develop those relationships early on that will last you a lifetime.

7. Find something you love to do

Find something that will help you wind down and de-stress at the end of the day. It can be exercise, sports, singing, painting, reading, or whatever you choose. Find something you are good at and enjoy doing. You will be happier and feel better about yourself when you are able to better yourself in the things you love to do.

8. Make the best of your situation

Know that there's always someone else who's worse off than you. You got a C on that Chemistry test? Well, someone else failed it. You broke your leg? Someone else doesn't have a leg. Remember that you have a *lot* compared to someone else. Don't dwell on the could-haves, the should-haves, the wishes, and the wants. Dwell on what can be done now, in the present time and place. There's no joy in what almost was.

9. Read positive and inspiring books

One of the best ways to maintain a positive attitude is by reading positive books. These books serve to encourage you, inspire you, and teach you. Reading requires that you sit still and focus, and by focusing on something positive, it helps you to keep a positive mind-set throughout the day.

10. Be thankful

Take some time and be thankful. Be thankful about what you have, who you are, and what your life is like. Think through all of the things that you can be thankful for. Even if you are going through a tough time in life, there are many things you have that you can be grateful for. You need to look for them and recognize them. The very act of focusing on what you are thankful for will help you maintain your positive attitude.

Try these suggestions out—even if you can only do one at a time, do them. Maybe do one a week until it becomes a habit. You will be happier in the long run. Always remember to give more than you take from others. If you do this with a positive attitude, I can promise you that you will not only change your life, but also that the lives of all the people that surround you as well.

I remember so many times in the hospital, and still along my journey, when I had to—and still have to—laugh. If I don't laugh at some of the things my body does, there is only one other thing I would do: cry. I didn't (and still don't) want to cry, so I've had to learn to laugh.

Elder Joseph B. Wirthlin said, "The way we react to adversity can be a major factor in how happy and successful we can be in life."[3]

The next time you're tempted to groan, you might try to laugh instead. It will extend your life and make the lives of all those around you more enjoyable.

Smile and be grateful, because life is beautiful.[4]

NOTES

1. Pages 89–93 adapted from Chad Hymas, *Doing What Must Be Done* (Salt Lake City: self published, 2011), 129–34.
2. Art Berg, *The Impossible Just Takes a Little Longer* (William Morrow Paperback, 2003).
3. Joseph B. Wirthlin, "Come What May, and Love It," *Ensign*, November 2008.
4. To learn more about Chad Hymas, visit his website chadhymas.com.

AL CARRAWAY, the award-winning LDS author of *More Than the Tattooed Mormon*, rounds out this pack of authors. Al was born and raised in Rochester, New York, where she became a member of The Church of Jesus Christ of Latter-day Saints in 2009. A well-known LDS speaker and blogger, Al's social presence first started with alfoxshead.blogspot.com, where she started blogging about her relationship with God in relation to her experiences and trials. Since then, Al has married her sweetheart, Ben, in the Oquirrh Mountain Temple, and now lives in Utah with him and their two kids, Gracie and Christian.

Al continues to blog and has now found herself traveling across the country every week to speak to LDS audiences of all kinds—at firesides, youth camps, and even prisons—sharing her conversion story and teaching all those who will listen.

THE SIMPLE THINGS

Al Carraway

Religion is only something people turn to when things are going wrong in their lives, right? Well, that's what I thought. And that wasn't me. In 2009, I had just graduated college. I was working full-time. I had an apartment all to myself. I was a stubborn New Yorker who thought I could do everything on my own. And I was *happy*. I didn't need help from anyone or anything, especially not religion.

I didn't grow up in the Church, and I definitely wasn't looking to join one. I met the missionaries as they were passing me on the sidewalk. I only listened to them because I told them I would if they brought me a steak to eat, thinking they wouldn't follow through. Joke's on me, because *they did*.

I had the elders over and let them talk to me about the gospel, simply because I felt obligated to. After all, they did bring me a steak.

I wanted to show them that the happiness and "the blessings" of the gospel they were teaching me about weren't real and it was all in their heads. I wanted to show them that they didn't actually need church—and I didn't either. But the only way to prove that to them was to do everything they taught me and show them that nothing would happen. I was going to pray, read scriptures every day, repent, and go to church, and I was going to do it long enough to allow the time for change and contrast to happen. I was going to give it a *real* try. You know, just to prove them wrong.

I joined the Church a few weeks before my 21st birthday, just two months after meeting the missionaries. Apparently, the joke was on me again. So, what happened? All I did was exactly what they taught me. All I did was pray. All I did was read the scriptures. All I did was go to church. And even though I started off with weird intentions, I was trying. We've been promised that if we *try*, and if we do those simple things of the gospel, we will become better.

Heavenly Father knew what I needed before I ever did.

Here I was, freshly baptized, finally knowing that there *is* a God, and feeling a happiness so overwhelming that I couldn't even try to compare it to anything I had *ever* felt before. It was a happiness that I have only felt when I'm doing those things God asks us to do. I may have thought I was happy before, but it was only because I didn't have anything to compare it to; I hadn't known any better. Happiness is fake and fleeting without God and His ways.

God is real, and His whole purpose is to give us the best ever created. What could go wrong? What happened next, after my baptism, wasn't anything I ever could have imagined or planned for.

If you've read my book, *More Than the Tattooed Mormon*, you'll know how hard things became because of my decision to join the Church. I lost every single one of my friends—they wanted *nothing* to do with me and what I was now a part of. My coworkers and my boss frequently got together just to scream at me and tell me how awful of a person I was and how what I was part of was wrong. They would make me watch all of these terrible and untrue videos about the gospel. (I didn't know what to do or how to defend the Church or even defend myself because I had only been a part of the Church for a few weeks; how small my knowledge was then!) I had *many* problems with my family, and was told by my dad—my absolute best friend—that he didn't want me as a daughter anymore. I didn't hear from him for years. I never could have imagined being asked by God to leave behind the only way I knew of living and move across the country to a place I had never been before (Utah) without knowing a single person or having a job lined up there, only to get there and be made an outcast. To be publicly and verbally shamed by strangers, *daily,* because of the way I looked. How hard that was, having just been baptized and feeling that I was being punished for doing what I thought was the right thing. And this was just the start of it.

I had no noteworthy trials before baptism, and now I was facing new ones *every day*: trials that never would have happened had I not joined the Church. I had never felt alone until I got baptized. I had never felt unaccepted and cast out until I joined the Church. I had never struggled with self-confidence until I joined the Church. I had never felt weak and abandoned until I joined the Church. I had never collapsed on the floor, *screaming* at God long enough to lose my voice because of how hard things were, until I joined the Church. I had never struggled in these ways before. Not until now.

It would have been easy to quit. Having just been baptized, it would have been very easy for me to give up and let things go back to how they used to be. It would have been easy to blame God. But I didn't. But, why didn't I? *Why keep going?*

Because I couldn't let a trial dim the truthfulness of the gospel. Because nothing I ever experienced could take away the *indescribable happiness* I had never before felt until I was living the way God asks—a *real* and *lasting* happiness that comes *only* from the gospel. Because I couldn't let a trial alter the unchanging truth that this is all *real*. We can never let a change of course alter the unchanging truth that God *is* taking care of us.

Even though I didn't have any friends or family to turn to after I was baptized, what I did have was the knowledge of what the elders had taught me—prayer, scriptures, and church. All I had was God. But in every situation, He is all you really need. When you know that God is real, and that lasting happiness comes only from the gospel, the only logical thing to do is to keep going with Him and asking for His help, instead of blaming Him or becoming angry. Once we make the decision to turn to God no matter what, our load becomes lighter.

It was those simple things of the gospel that helped me through my hardest trials. It was through my honest pleas to God that strength and comfort came—comfort that can be felt *during* the hard times. It was talking to God that brought me light in the darkness. It was through the Book of Mormon that I was able to hear counsel and guidance. It was church that brought me strength when I was weak.

In 2015, two missionaries and their investigator video-chatted with me. Their investigator had been wondering what to do with his life, what to do with God, and what church he should attend. I could feel my testimony growing stronger as I watched the elders teach with the Spirit, offering perfect responses to this man's questions.

Yet, regardless of our best efforts, he decided he had given up on his quest, and no longer wanted to learn about this church because of his lack of answers. He said it wasn't for him. Then, after the closing prayer, he revealed that he hadn't prayed in months and hadn't even made it through a chapter of the scriptures.

I wish so badly I could have asked him right at the beginning of the lesson, "Are you praying? Are you reading the Book of Mormon?" And when he had said no, I could have easily said, with a confident smile, "that's your problem."

How can we expect answers when we aren't turning to God? How can He answer us when we don't speak to Him? When we don't ask Him? When we don't read His words and counsel in the scriptures? How can we expect anyone to help us when we aren't doing anything to receive that help?

An old bishop I had several years ago told me something I'll never forget. He said he has yet to have someone who reads their scriptures and prays daily walk in his office having already decided that the Church wasn't for them.

How can we think the gospel isn't for us if we aren't learning about it and *living* it? How can we make that decision if we don't actually know what the gospel really is? We can't.

Are you without a testimony? Or, if you have one, is it weak? Trials are the perfect thing to fix that! It is the chance for us to finally do those things we have been taught, and to allow ourselves to let God help and show us what He can do for us when we turn to Him. God *wants* to help you. He loves you.

Whether you grew up in the Church or not, testimony or not, we must all make the effort to find out if the gospel is true and if we should live it. How do we do that? The exact way I did. It is through *acting* and following through. It is through our efforts of trying, not perfection, that we are blessed. It is through the simple things we were taught first (prayer, scripture reading, church attendance, repentance, and faith), whether in Primary or by missionaries, that we are blessed. And why are we taught them first? Because the power that comes from doing those things is not wishful thinking, it's *real*.

When hard times come, when questions and doubts arise, when things seem a little off, the first thing to do is evaluate ourselves and our efforts. Are we actually doing the simple things of the gospel? Are we praying throughout the day? When was the last time we read our scriptures? Do we read them *consistently*? Are we going to church? Are we repenting?

Are we allowing God to help us by doing the things He asks of us? Are we doing these things long enough to allow that contrast and change to happen?

It's too bad that complaining about our trials, doubts, or questions doesn't get us anywhere, because I think we would all make pretty impressive progress, if that were the case. When things become hard or confusing, it's easy to spend our time just *thinking* about how badly things stink right now and how we wish things were different. But, unfortunately, such thoughts are not productive and will not change anything. We must act. We must do.

PRAYER

I had never said a prayer in my entire life until the elders asked me to start. I had no idea how to pray, and it was incredibly awkward for me. Not only did I not know how or what to say, but the idea of talking out loud to a God I didn't even know existed at the time seemed a lot like having a conversation with myself. I had a church pamphlet that the missionaries had given me that had instructions on the back, in bullet points, about how to pray. I would pray with one eye closed and the other eye on the pamphlet because I didn't even know how to start a prayer.

But the more I did it, the more comfortable it became. And I learned firsthand that *every* single prayer is heard when it's done with real intent. It was through my awkward prayers that I was able to know and feel that there really is a God. I could see solutions, opportunities, and blessings in my everyday life that showed me that not only is He there, but that He cares.

He cares about me. He cares about the simplest of things that matter to me. I can count on one hand how many times Heavenly Father actually spoke in the scriptures. It is usually His Son—Jesus Christ—or the Spirit who speaks. But every one of us can speak to God directly. How cool and sacred is that?

I also learned, repeatedly, that specific prayers receive specific answers. Regardless of how you feel—confused, hurt, mad, alone—tell Him *everything*. Honest prayers are *crucial*. They're crucial for conversion. They're crucial for receiving answers. They're crucial for receiving comfort and strength. They're crucial to build up a real and lasting relationship with God that will help you through absolutely anything life brings your way. When you close your eyes to pray, picture Him standing right in front of you. Talk to Him like you would a real person, because the reality is, He is.

Force yourself to say a prayer no matter how frustrated you are. Pray hardest when it's hardest to pray. It was in my honest prayers that I received more detailed comfort and counsel through all of my trials. It's important to vent and open up fully and completely to your Father in Heaven. But it is crucial to listen—and not just listen to what *we* want to hear.

Sometimes I have no idea what I should be asking Heavenly Father for during a trial. A trick I've learned, is asking God for help with my prayers. When you start your prayer, simply ask, "Heavenly Father, help me with this prayer," and then continue speaking to Him. Every time I have done this, I have found myself asking for things I never thought of—things that were completely inspired and His will.

It's not often that I check my messages on Instagram (for several reasons), and it's pretty rare that I respond, *especially* to contentious messages about me or the Church. But I just happened to check my messages one day, and read one from a fourteen-year-old girl I did not know who follows my posts. She wrote two large paragraphs cussing me out and cussing out the Church. She was an active member as far as attendance goes, but went to church only because of her parents. I didn't even know how to begin to address everything she had yelled at me about, so I just closed out of the message and thought I'd leave it at that. But I couldn't stop thinking about her. I reopened her message later that day, and the next thing I knew, I gave her my cell phone number and we were texting. What? I know. So weird. After over an hour of her opening up to me with her struggles and feelings, she told me that she had just barely said a prayer: her first prayer in a long time, and perhaps her first *honest* prayer ever. Immediately after she told me this, her language and tone completely changed. She confessed that her prayer had left her in tears. She was able to feel peace and comfort for the *"first time"* in a long time. She confessed that she had felt God there for her.

The very next day, she texted me first thing in the morning. She was still super-positive and hopeful about her challenges, just as she'd been the night before. Unfortunately, only two hours later that same day, she started cussing me out again, questioning God and His hand in her life.

Are we allowing the adversary to let us overlook and dismiss those sweet experiences and bring us away from God? Do we expect help to come in a certain or specific way that *we* had in mind? Are we failing to recognize the unsuspected help and guidance from people, resources, or feelings? The adversary knows when we have spiritual experiences and will be right there to try and rob us of the light and progress we receive. One of his greatest tools is doubt. "Did I really feel that way?" "Did that actually happen?" Sometimes we wonder where God is and why He doesn't help or answer us. Truth is, when we turn to Him, He always does—just like that girl who was brought to tears when she prayed because of the comfort of His presence and spirit that surrounded her.

It is important to note that Satan most often gets to us by our thoughts. He is the one that tells us that we can't pray, that we are not worthy to talk to God, or that God is not listening. He is the one that tells us we don't have time to read, or that Church is too long or not important. Do not listen. Do not let Satan win. It's easier to recognize the adversary when we ask ourselves, "Is this preventing me from doing the right thing? Is this preventing me from turning to God?"

SCRIPTURES

Before my baptism, I would read the scriptures every day because the elders asked me to, but they made *no sense* to me at first. Every time I would think, "what on earth did I just read?" I can't say that I recognized any answers I had from reading at first; *but*, though I didn't recognize any answers at first, every single time I read, strength and comfort and the Spirit were there to help me in every situation. The language definitely becomes more familiar and more natural as we read.

After losing friends and family, those simple things were all I had to turn to. Every time things got hard, I would spend every single *second* that I had free reading the Book of Mormon. I had a copy of the Book of Mormon everywhere—one in my car, one in my purse, and even one I would sneak into the front of my pants at work, and I would fake bathroom breaks just so I could read for a minute in the bathroom stall. I would read it on all of my work breaks, and while I was just walking.

Yeah, it was *hard* feeling alone in my trials, *but* I did have a copy of the Book of Mormon with me to read every day, everywhere I went. Not once did my situation change because of it—not really—but every single time, I would receive strength and knowledge to be able to handle what I was going through. Sometimes we don't read a verse that speaks directly to our situation, but it's really important to note that even if that does happen, every time we read, strength and guidance will come to us. That is a promised blessing from reading His word. It comes from the act of turning to Him. I don't know what I'd have done without that book. That is where strength and happiness comes from. Scriptures truly do heal a hurting heart and a wounded soul, and help us in the trickiest of situations.

I cannot count how many times I've finished Book of Mormon or Doctrine and Covenants. And I don't write that to brag, I write that because I seriously rely on them so much. Those books are my life. Because, simply put, without them, I am not. I am not strong. I am not confident. I am not wise or smart. I am not guided. I am not *me*.

Guys, I get you stubborn, independent folks—I was a twenty-one-year-old New Yorker who thought I could conquer the world on my own. But if it weren't for giving the Book of Mormon a *real* chance every day (even when it didn't make sense to me at first, and even though I didn't really want to), I wouldn't be here. I wouldn't have what I do. I would not truly be happy. I would not truly be me without it. Without Him. And I hope that each of you will give the Book of Mormon a real effort and allow yourself to be changed and blessed the way I have been. This is *real life*, guys. Real-life strength. Real-life promises. Real-life God.

To get more out of scripture reading, it needs to be partnered with prayer. Ask God for the Spirit before you start reading. Ask Him any personal questions you have. Ask Him for the Spirit to help strengthen, speak, teach, and comfort you. The Book of Mormon was written for *us*. As you read, ask yourself, "How does this apply to *me* right now?" Having that mind-set and perspective will unfold a new world of power to you as you look to apply scripture stories to your personal life.

I definitely know it's not about how fast we get through them, but knowing the strength and revelation that comes from reading, it should be about how often we read; so we can receive even more strength and revelation to help us in the best way. The reality is we have a spirit living inside of us and it's crucial to feed it.

Here are five easy things to do to feed our spirit:

1. Read every day. Set a specific time to read that will work for your daily schedule, and make it a habit. It could be lunchtime, or before school or work—even if it means setting your alarm a little bit earlier. I prefer to read as soon as I wake up, when the world is quiet, but the Spirit is not—breakfast for me and breakfast for my soul!

2. Don't limit yourself on how much to read. Instead of saying "I'll read X amount of verses a day" and then stop, just read until you can't anymore, for whatever reason.

3. It's okay to read more than once a day. What? I know. And it will be a huge contrast in yourself and your life when you do this. And do you know how much you can gain if you watch just one less episode on Netflix and read instead? Or how much you can get from a few verses while you're waiting for your water to boil? Or waiting in the car for your friend to come outside?

4. Keep a Book of Mormon everywhere. I know a lot of you are big on the Gospel Library App, which is great, but I'm talkin' hard copies, so you can actually see your scriptures and be reminded of them in times when you wouldn't otherwise. (You can get them for free from the missionaries, or if you live in highly populated member areas, DI and thrift stores have some awesome vintage ones from the '70s for a quarter). Keep one in your bathroom, one on your kitchen counter, and one by your bedside (pocket-sized ones are perfect for your car and your backpack or purse).

5. Start over. When you finish, celebrate and be excited! Soak it in. Gloat a little, even to yourself, for accomplishing

it. But then turn it right back to page one, and start from the beginning. A week or a month or until the start of next year are not appropriate lengths for parties.

CHURCH

The first time I went to church, I hated it. I felt uncomfortable the second I walked in. I didn't look or dress like anyone else there. I thought that people could smell that I didn't belong there somehow. I told the elders I would never go back, and I meant it. Yet there I was exactly a week later, standing in front of my closet, realizing I still didn't have a dress to wear to sacrament meeting. Before I knew what I was doing, I was already on my way back to church.

My second time back was much different. This time I didn't worry about fitting in or what people might be thinking about me. I went for answers. I went to test promises that were made to me, not just by the elders, but by God—promises of strength and comfort and knowledge and renewal. And because I went for *me*, I was focused and I was filled with the Spirit. And because I went with faith that those promises would be fulfilled, they were.

How is your church experience? Are you going to church regularly? Are you staying for all three hours? Are you going for you, or because your parents make you? Are you there grudgingly? During church, where are your thoughts? Are you focused? Are you on your phone? Are you praying to God and renewing your commitment to Him when the sacrament is being passed?

You will not receive the blessings of church when your mind is elsewhere. Next Sunday, go for *you*. Go with the mindset that a specific answer to your prayers *will* be there. When we go seeking to listen and find strength, *we will* find. God Himself promises us that.

To all those who feel they do not fit in, I tell you from hurtful experience and with confidence, you're wrong. These blessings and promises are for you. You belong here; you are a part of this! This gospel is for *you*. Embrace your differences, knowing that you were created and crafted by our perfect God, a God who makes no mistakes. To all those who are afraid to return because of past mistakes, I say, come! Do not hold yourself back from the best blessings any longer. To all those who may have become distant due to being offended, I ask, is it still worth it? Is it worth giving up your eternal happiness over it?

REPENTANCE

That word, I think, just paints a negative picture in our heads, doesn't it? It sometimes, unconsciously, makes us feel that we are a bad person because it implies we're doing something wrong. Right? Well, no. It simply means change. Repentance is not punishment or condemnation; it's optimistic and completely positive! It means we *can* become better. We *can* become who we were meant to be all along—the person God wants *you* to be. And isn't that the greatest gift to be given?

Some things we need to repent of are easier than other things. It can be done in our nighttime prayers: when we recognize what we could have done better that day, and then asking for forgiveness—committing to do a little better the next day. Perhaps that means treating someone a little better. Maybe it means we could have done a little more to help out our parents.

Other times, it will take confronting another person or meeting with our bishop. If Christ said He was coming tomorrow, imagine how long the line would be to see your bishop, and by then it would be too late. Don't carry unnecessary things. It will weigh you down and make other things in your life harder to handle. Don't put off what can and should be done now.

Will it take effort? Yeah. Will it be worth it? *Profoundly.* Everlastingly. The steps we need to take and the changes we need to make are worth *every* sacrifice. But, is it really a sacrifice when we are getting *more* in return? That's what Christ does for us. President Monson implored, "I plead with you to correct your mistakes. Our Savior died to provide you and me that blessed gift."[1]

You may feel that you are alone, or that no one knows how you feel. Thoughts that no one cares about you or what you're going through are wrong. Thoughts that you are "too far gone" to change or to receive God's help are wrong. They are from the adversary. *Do not listen.* How someone else acts toward you doesn't change that. Let others do and act and react however they want. Because that won't ever change the fact that the most powerful being to ever exist is always there for *you.* Always. Whatever you may be going through *does* matter to Him, because *you* matter to Him. When speaking as the

Savior, Elder Bradley D. Foster said, "I've been where you are, I know what comes next, and I'll help you through it."[2]

Make taking care of yourself a priority. It may be a slow process, but giving up won't get you there any quicker. Do not look back. You aren't going that way. Don't let who you used to be hold you back from who you can become. "How is it that ye have forgotten that the Lord is able to do all things?" (1 Nephi 7:12). Now is not the time for God to judge you, but to help you. He wants you back. He misses you even when you are a little bit distant from Him. And if you think Heavenly Father will do anything to stop you from being happy and returning to Him, you're wrong. You are not alone. Help is there because Christ is there next to you. He doesn't just stand there with you; He feels with you.

God is for us. So it doesn't matter who is against us.

FAITH

It's silly to expect to avoid trials simply because of our membership in the Church. When turning to Him and living His commandments, we are, however, prevented from experiencing many needless and *unnecessary* trials.

Not long ago I was going through a really hard trial. It was the kind of trial that lasts much longer than you think it should have. I'd like to say I was as strong as I was when it first presented itself, but I wasn't. It was the type of trial where your strength is worn very thin and you feel like you've been positive about it for too long; you can't help but let tears stream down your face during random parts of your day and question what else you could be doing that you're not already doing to make it go away.

And usually in those tough trials, the answer that you can't be doing anything else is harder to hear. It's hardest to hear that we are doing all that we can and we just need to *endure*. Most times I feel like I have enough faith to be helped or healed right then in that very second. I do. I feel like I am immovable when it comes to knowing of His miracles and power. But do we have the faith to *not* be helped or healed right then? Do we have the faith to let Him *not* solve or heal right away? Do we have the faith to stay faithful when we feel our faith has been stretched thin? Do we have the faith to last long, long months and know that no matter our trials or change of course or the time frame given, it does not alter the unchanging truth that God is taking care of us?

I eventually get there. But it's not until after I have moved beyond the feeling that I have been "faithful enough for long enough" and that I should have earned myself a solution by now. It sometimes takes a few breakdowns of me crying and literally yelling at God to get there. And that's okay.

Because it's through my honest yelling and crying to God of what I'm really thinking that I make progress with Him, my situation, and mostly myself. It's where I accept and feel that I won't drown even if the trials won't go away quite yet. It's where I accept that sometimes all the answers won't be there, but comfort and strength always will be, because God will always be there.

Here's my key to finding strength *during* the thick of hard times:

First: Am I doing the simple things of the gospel?

Second: *So be it.*

The Spirit spoke this so boldly to me in a previous trial while I was reading the scriptures. "They brought their wives and children together, and whosoever believed . . . in the word of God they caused that they should be cast into the fire. . . . Now Amulek said unto Alma: Behold, perhaps they will burn us also. And Alma said: *Be it according to the will of the Lord*" (Alma 14:8, 12–13; emphasis added).

Surely if Alma could trust Heavenly Father so much with his life and be able to have so much desire to follow His will that he could so easily and calmly say, "*so be it*," surely I could be confident with the trials given to me: that no matter what, I can understand that it is the Lord's will for me. And that's ultimately what I want in all circumstances. I don't want it if He doesn't want it for me. Isn't it so silly how hard it is for us to allow His will to take over? Like, why wouldn't we want it to go the way our perfect God wants it to go?

I have learned and relearned that sometimes God asks us to do hard things. Sometimes He asks us to leave our family and move across the country, as He did for me. Sometimes He asks us to lose all our friends and be persecuted. Sometimes He doesn't give us all the answers and allows us to walk blindfolded, holding His hand. But the blessings He gives us in return are always greater than what we knew was even available for us.

I have learned too many times that although nothing goes the way I want it to and pray for it to, it has always been *profoundly better* than what I even knew was available for myself. All trials and course changes have led me to better things and bigger blessings. Every. Single. Time. There is always great comfort in His will, no matter how unwanted or hard it may be. Knowing that God is real, and that the gospel is true means that your life will never be the same. But *always* better.

Sometimes we can't help but think how much easier it would be if things had gone the way we wanted them to go. But little do we know what's right around the corner for us when we choose to remember and follow God—the opportunities that await, the people, the growth, and the blessings. It's there. Hard? Yes, undoubtedly. Worth it? Absolutely and profoundly. But fear, confusion, or anger should never be an option for us once we remember who is guiding us. Your prayers have been heard. But greater are the things He has in store for you. Receive the unexpected, but profoundly greater path with the best blessings.

I'm grateful that we aren't asked to be strong all the time. But we are asked to be faithful and hopeful—to not shut Him out, but to allow Him to help us. I'm especially grateful for the comfort we can feel in the darkest of times, and the peace we can feel in the hardest of times. Peace in knowing that He is in control. Comfort and peace are always there because Christ is always there.

Maybe that's what I love most about the gospel. Not that it prevents us from the blows of life, but that we can feel an incredible peace and love in every dark moment. Do not be captured by trends. Do not let temporary challenges make you forget that which is lasting. Look beyond present-day challenges; there is so much more beyond this life.

No matter who we are or what we're going through, there is always a solution. It is, and always will be, Christ. The gospel is not our last option; it is our only option. It's how and why we are here. Giving up is not an option, and it never can be. No matter how hard things get, or how easy it would be to give up and go back to where things were comfortable, it cannot change the fact that this gospel is real. He is real. His promises are real. And this happiness is real. And our forever depends upon how we choose to act today. Embrace the unexpected, knowing it is guided by the most powerful and all-knowing Being to ever exist. He exists for us. He exists for you. He exists to see you succeed, be truly happy, and return.

We find whatever it is we're looking for. Look for the good. Look for Him. Do not worry over things you have no control over. Refuse negative thoughts—do not justify the adversary in your thinking because you "expect" him to be there in trials. Do not let time and trials dim your faith or diminish the truthfulness of His promises to you. Refrain from thinking that God doesn't care or that you will be shortchanged from the absolute best. Trust God with your life. After all, He's the one who gave it to you.

So, next time we find ourselves on our floor yelling at God and pleading for things to be over and for things to be different, I hope that we can take a quick break from how we think our lives should go, and with hope say, "so be it." Because our trials and our change of course will never alter the unchanging truth that God is leading us to the best blessings. Why stop when we can keep going?

We are given everything to succeed. We have been given a God. Don't deny yourself the best things by putting off talking to Him or reading the scriptures. Do not lose sight of the simple things of the gospel. Because the gospel is beautiful.

NOTES

1. Thomas S. Monson, "The Three Rs of Choice," *Ensign*, November 2010.
2. Bradley D. Foster, "It's Never Too Early and It's Never Too Late," *Ensign*, November 2015.

ABOUT THE COMPILER

ELISE HAHL is a freelance editor and writer, born to parents who taught her to love classy Jane Austen novels and the even-classier Philadelphia Phillies. She served a mission in Brazil, studied English at Stanford, and went on to earn an MA in nonfiction writing at Johns Hopkins. Most recently, she was a compiler and coeditor for *Do Not Attempt in Heels: Mission Stories and Advice from Sisters Who've Been There*.

Elise lives in Pittsburgh with her husband, Oliver, and their five children, who root for the Pirates and don't really get the whole Phillies thing. She loves them anyway.